Bridging the Gap between Machine and Language using First-Class Building Blocks

Inauguraldissertation
der Philosophisch-naturwissenschaftlichen Fakultät
der Universität Bern

vorgelegt von

Toon Verwaest

von Belgien

Leiter der Arbeit:
Prof. Dr. O. Nierstrasz
Institut für Informatik und angewandte Mathematik

Von der Philosophisch-naturwissenschaftlichen Fakultät angenommen.

Copyright © 2012 Toon Verwaest.

Software Composition Group
University of Bern
Institute of Computer Science and Applied Mathematics
Neubrückstrasse 10
CH-3012 Bern
http://scg.unibe.ch/

ISBN: 978-1-105-51835-5

 This work is licensed under the *Creative Commons Attribution–ShareAlike 3.0 License*. The license is available at http://creativecommons.org/licenses/by-sa/3.0/.

This dissertation is available at http://scg.unibe.ch.

Acknowledgments

My adventure in Bern started more than four years ago, in October 2007. This page is too short to capture the gratitude I have towards all those who have contributed in any way to this dissertation.

First I'd like to extend my gratitude to Oscar Nierstrasz for supporting me throughout my time at the Software Composition Group. He gave me the freedom to develop my own research project, and provided invaluable support in formulating my thoughts. It is thanks to his well-organized research group that developing this thesis almost seemed effortless.

I thank Marcus Denker for his continued support and interest in my work. I very much enjoyed our discussions about research; especially while exploring the Swiss mountains. I'd like to thank him for reviewing this thesis, writing the Koreferat, and accepting to be on the PhD committee.

I thank Torsten Braun for accepting to chair the PhD defense.

I am especially grateful to my bachelor student Olivier Flückiger, and master students Camillo Bruni and David Gurtner for the many weeks we have spent discussing, and programming on Pinocchio. Without your optimism and input this thesis would not have been possible!

I am much obliged to my co-authors Camillo Bruni, David Gurtner, Adrian Lienhard, Oscar Nierstrasz, Mircea Lungu, Niko Schwarz, Erwann Wernli, and Olivier Flückiger for the stressful days (and nights) writing the papers that formed the base of this dissertation.

I would like to thank Camillo Bruni, Erwann Wernli, Olivier Flückiger, and Niko Schwartz for struggling through earlier drafts of this dissertation, and for helping to shape it into what it is today.

I thank all former and current members of the Software Composition Group: Marcus Denker, Tudor Gîrba, Orla Greevy, Adrian Kuhn, Adrian Lienhard, Mircea Lungu, Fabrizio Perin, Lukas Renggli, Jorge Ressia, David Röthlisberger, Niko Schwarz, and Erwann Wernli. I thank Gabriela Arévalo for introducing me to this wonderful group. I am thankful to Therese Schmidt, and especially to Iris Keller, for taking almost all administrative tasks of my shoulders.

I thank my bachelor students Daniel Langone, Camillo Bruni, and master student Sandro De Zanet, for the fun projects we worked on.

I am thankful to my *Hilfsassistants* Camillo Bruni for the *Programming Languages* lecture, and Raffael Krebs for the *Compiler Construction* lecture, for greatly reducing my additional workload.

I thank my friend Adrian Kuhn for the hours of hacking (and drinking) together, especially during the first year of my PhD.

I am grateful to my parents for believing in me, for their support, and especially for the many nice visits.

I thank my dear friends Sandro De Zanet, Raffael Krebs, and Camillo Bruni for the many dinners, drinks, games, days of skiing, hikes, *etc.* You have made my stay in Switzerland a pleasant one!

Above all, I'm indebted to Laura Sánchez Serrano for joining me in Bern, and for sticking through yet another thesis. I thank her for supporting me, taking over chores, and listening to me complain during the writing phase; but also for the many adventures we have lived together.

Toon Verwaest
February 20, 2012

Abstract

High-performance virtual machines (VMs) are increasingly reused for programming languages for which they were not initially designed. Unfortunately, VMs are usually tailored to specific languages, offer only a very limited interface to running applications, and are closed to extensions. As a consequence, extensions required to support new languages often entail the construction of custom VMs, thus impacting reuse, compatibility and performance. Short of building a custom VM, the language designer has to choose between the expressiveness and the performance of the language. In this dissertation we argue that the best way to open the VM is to eliminate it. We present Pinocchio, a natively compiled Smalltalk, in which we identify and reify three basic building blocks for object-oriented languages.

First we define a protocol for message passing similar to calling conventions, independent of the actual *message lookup* mechanism. The lookup is provided by a self-supporting runtime library written in Smalltalk and compiled to native code. Since it unifies the meta- and base-level we obtain a metaobject protocol (MOP).

Then we decouple the language-level manipulation of state from the machine-level implementation by extending the structural reflective model of the language with *object layouts*, *layout scopes* and *slots*.

Finally we reify behavior using AST nodes and *first-class interpreters* separate from the low-level language implementation.

We describe the implementations of all three first-class building blocks. For each of the blocks we provide a series of examples illustrating how they enable typical extensions to the runtime, and we provide benchmarks validating the practicality of the approaches.

Contents

1 Introduction   **1**
  1.1 Contributions 3
  1.2 Outline 4

2 Object-Oriented Building Blocks   **7**
  2.1 Communication: Efficient Message Dispatch 7
      2.1.1 Lookup Cache 8
      2.1.2 Virtual Method Tables 8
      2.1.3 Inline Caches 8
      2.1.4 Method Inlining 10
      2.1.5 Customization 11
  2.2 Data: Object Format and Management 11
      2.2.1 Hardware Constraints 12
      2.2.2 Garbage Collection Constraints 13
  2.3 Code: Method Structure 15
      2.3.1 AST 15
      2.3.2 Bytecode 16
      2.3.3 Threaded Code 17
      2.3.4 Native Code 20
  2.4 Code: Method Behavior 20
      2.4.1 Recursive interpretation 21
      2.4.2 Manual stack management 21
      2.4.3 Stack-mapped context frame 22
      2.4.4 Register-Based Execution 23
  2.5 Summary 23

3 Background and Problems   **25**
  3.1 Reflection 25
      3.1.1 Discrete and Continuous Behavioral Reflection 26
      3.1.2 Separation of base and meta-level 27
      3.1.3 Partial Behavioral Reflection 27
      3.1.4 High-level reflective API 28
      3.1.5 AOP 29
  3.2 Generating Tailored Virtual Machines 29
  3.3 Problem 1: The Tyranny of a Closed VM 30
  3.4 Problem 2: Low-level Object Structure 32

		3.5	Problem 3: Low-Level Execution Model	33
		3.6	Summary	34
4	**First-Class Message Lookup**			**35**
	4.1	The Message is the Medium		36
	4.2	See Pinocchio Run		38
		4.2.1	Invocation Conventions	39
		4.2.2	Lookup and Apply	39
		4.2.3	Avoiding Meta-regression	41
		4.2.4	Separation of Class and Behavior	42
		4.2.5	Native Compilation	42
		4.2.6	Bootstrapping Pinocchio	44
		4.2.7	Performance	45
		4.2.8	Metrics	46
	4.3	Evaluation and applications		46
		4.3.1	Reconfiguring the meta-level	47
		4.3.2	Changing lookup semantics	49
	4.4	Discussion		49
	4.5	Related Work		52
	4.6	Summary		53
5	**First-Class Object Layouts**			**55**
	5.1	Flexible Object Layouts in a Nutshell		56
	5.2	First-Class Slots		58
		5.2.1	Primitive Slots	59
		5.2.2	Customized Slots	60
		5.2.3	Virtual Slots	65
		5.2.4	Implementation and Performance	66
	5.3	First-Class Layout Scopes		67
		5.3.1	Bit Field Layout Scope	67
		5.3.2	Property Layout Scope	69
	5.4	Stateful Traits		72
		5.4.1	Traits	73
		5.4.2	Stateful Traits	74
		5.4.3	Installing State of Stateful Traits	74
		5.4.4	Installing Behavior of Stateful Traits	76
	5.5	Inspecting Objects		76
	5.6	Dynamic Structure Modifications		77
		5.6.1	Modification Model	77
		5.6.2	Building and Installing	78
		5.6.3	Pharo Class Installer	79
		5.6.4	Metrics	80
	5.7	Related Work		80
		5.7.1	Language Extensions	81
		5.7.2	Meta Modeling	81
		5.7.3	Annotations	82

		5.7.4	Object Relational Mapping	82
		5.7.5	First-Class Slots	83
		5.7.6	Unified Slots and Methods	83
		5.7.7	Dynamic Software Update	84
	5.8	Summary		84

6 First-Class Interpreters — 87

- 6.1 First-Class Interpreters in a Nutshell 88
- 6.2 Implementing Custom Interpreters 90
  - 6.2.1 A Simple Debugger 90
  - 6.2.2 Alias Interpreter 92
  - 6.2.3 Recursive Interpreters 97
- 6.3 Minimizing the Interpreter Stack 102
- 6.4 Performance 103
- 6.5 Related Work 104
  - 6.5.1 Tower Approach to First-Class Interpreters 104
  - 6.5.2 Meta-circular Interpreters 105
  - 6.5.3 Dealing with Infinity 105
- 6.6 Summary 106

7 Conclusions — 107

- 7.1 Future Work 108
  - 7.1.1 Research Directions 108
  - 7.1.2 Practical Steps 109

Bibliography — 111

1
Introduction

Initial prototypes of programming languages are easily implemented as abstract syntax tree (AST) interpreters written in high-level languages. Nevertheless, evolving these implementations into efficient interoperable runtimes requires a large development effort and deep knowledge of compiler optimization techniques. This has spawned a lot of research to reduce the cost by reusing existing language implementations.

At the top layer, dynamic programming languages often provide bendable semantics that are used to modify the language from within. Reflection is a well-studied technique that allows programs to inspect and modify their own structure and behavior. It provides a window into the internal structure and execution details of the language from within the language. This makes it a key component for *self-sustainability*, the evolution of a language from within. Extensive meta programming facilities are introduced which let users tailor a language to their needs, ranging from Java annotations [138] to full-blown language workbenches such as Helvetia [122] and SugarJ [52]. Reflection is mostly implemented as an add-on to programming languages, rendering it unable to modify the underlying runtime implementation. For example if we would like to change the method lookup semantics in standard Smalltalk implementations, we can at most emulate the new semantics on top of the standard virtual machine (VM) in terms of the old semantics. This imposes a performance and memory penalty, and makes it clear that reflection can only go so far without proper support from the underlying implementation.

In the middle layer, virtual machines for object-oriented languages are typically programmed using a fixed set of bytecodes. This provides a degree of freedom since the bytecodes might provide a more adaptable language than the language it supports. This approach is for example taken by Groovy [66], jRuby [82], Scala [128], *etc.*, targeting the Java VM (JVM). Nevertheless these VMs are typically sealed from the language they support. The bytecodes are designed specifically for a particular language and its current language features. An alien VM exhibits limitations and baked-in assumptions originating from the original language, obstructing the efficient implementation of the new language. New languages cannot extend the capabilities of a VM from within the runtime.

At the bottom layer, some VMs are constructed so that they can easily be adapted. They are constructed in a meta-circular fashion [78, 80, 143], built from reusable components [70], or generated from high-level models [123]. The resulting VMs are still sealed from the language they support however. Any application running on top of the resulting VM is limited to the features that were chosen for a given compiled version of the VM. This is a problem especially if a combination of two conflicting extensions is required.

In summary, a language designer works either on top of the VM using either the language or bytecode, and is limited to emulation and simulation of unsupported features, or he changes the VM itself which forces him to abandon compatibility. This indicates the need for adaptable, reconfigurable and retargetable runtime support.

We state our thesis as follows:

Thesis:

To make object-oriented language implementations reusable we need to reify three fundamental building blocks (1) the communication between objects, (2) the gap between the system-level and language-level view of data, and (3) the interpretation of code.

In this dissertation we argue that the best way to open the VM is to eliminate it. Instead, we identify three fundamental building blocks of object-oriented runtimes, and describe how to build up an open runtime from the bottom up by relying on those building blocks:

Communication. To promote freedom of language on a per-object basis we divide method invocation into two parts: a message passing protocol and a reified *message lookup* mechanism.

The message passing protocol reuses the native application binary interface (ABI) calling conventions as the most basic mechanism of communication. By using native function calls to implement message sending, we limit the assumptions about language used by the target object to a bare minimum, and we maintain interoperability with ABI compatible applications.

On top of this messaging protocol, we provide a library for Smalltalk lookup semantics. It is implemented as a self-supporting runtime library compiled to native code, while maintaining the standard polymorphic behavior of Smalltalk at the meta-level. Since it unifies the meta- and base-level, we obtain a metaobject protocol (MOP). Infinite meta-recursion is avoided by using pre-filled inline caches.

Data. To increase the expressiveness of the programming language in terms of its object structure, we decouple the language-level manipulation of state from the machine-level implementation. We extend the structural reflective model of the language with *object layouts*, *layout scopes* and *slots*, allowing programmers to build objects in terms of high-level reusable object fragments rather than being limited by simple object extension through subclassing.

Code. To ease language experimentation and debugging, we reify behavior using AST nodes and *first-class interpreters* separate from the low-level language implementation. Instead of requiring complex code transformations or needing to modify a low-level VM, first-class interpreters support light-weight language extensions through subclassing.

We provide separate implementations of the first-class building blocks and show how they are beneficial for the evolution of the runtime by making it more customizable and easier to debug.

1.1 Contributions

1. *Unified meta- and base-level*
   By generating the whole runtime from a high-level meta-circular specification that is formally late-bound, we attain polymorphism at the meta-level. The use of the same language for both the meta-level as well as the base-level ensures that meta-programs are as reconfigurable as normal base-level applications. In Chapter 4, we will illustrate the flexibility of the model by implementing a method tracer and a prototype-based language.

2. *Customizable object layouts*
   We specify a framework for defining custom layouts of objects built from a set of basic building blocks that have an implicit hardware specification. This allows language developers to build elaborate object models without having to hook into the compiler, while giving greater customization power to developers with high performance or low memory requirements. In Chapter 5, we exemplify this approach by presenting a typical set of use-cases, including a hybrid between Smalltalk-80 arrayed objects and Python-style hash-table objects. This work has first appeared in [146].

3. *Customizable dynamic code update mechanism*
   We provide a single central interface that combines both the compiler

and the class installer infrastructure so that they can be customized. This serves as entry point for building dynamic code update mechanisms that are required to support more elaborate schemes of application and language evolution. We show the usefulness of our model by drastically improving the performance of the Pharo[1] class builder. This work has first appeared in [147].

4. *First-class interpreters*
 By introducing first-class meta-circular interpreters to the runtime we provide a clear object-oriented interface to building custom interpreters. This is especially useful for building interpreters with lower performance but higher flexibility requirements such as customizable debuggers. In Chapter 6, we show how this setup can be used to easily implement elaborate debugger support such as the *object-flow debugger* [92]. This work has first appeared in [145].

We provide implementations of the contributions in two different systems:

Pinocchio is a Smalltalk in which different execution styles have been prototyped. It implements AST, bytecode, and direct-threaded interpretation using stack-based opcodes, and native compilation targeting register-based hardware. First-class interpreters are implemented in the interpreter flavors of Pinocchio, whereas unification of the meta- and base-level have been explored in the native compiled version.

All versions are bootstrapped by cross-compilation from Pharo Smalltalk [15]. While being an experimental runtime with few implemented primitives, it is practically usable as standard Smalltalk environment with competitive dynamic language performance.

PlayOut is an implementation of customizable object layouts on top of Pharo Smalltalk and Helvetia [122]. PlayOut requires no changes to the Pharo VM while exhibiting no negative performance impact.

1.2 Outline

This dissertation is structured as follows:

Chapter 2 identifies three fundamental building blocks of object-oriented languages. It provides an overview of low-level implementation details for these building blocks, and their implications for the resulting runtimes.

Chapter 3 gives an overview of the related work. In particular we describe the state of the art in meta-circular VMs and object-oriented reflection. We then discuss the problems with those approaches.

---

[1] http://www.pharo-project.org

Chapter 4 replaces the traditional VM with a native communication interface for objects. We describe Pinocchio, the implementation of our prototype that implements a self-supporting runtime library for Smalltalk. The runtime library itself is also implemented in Smalltalk and unifies the meta-level with the base-level such that objects from either level are indistinguishable. This provides Smalltalk-based objects with a compiler-generated metaobject protocol.

Chapter 5 introduces *layouts*, *layout scopes* and *slots* as structural abstractions used by language tools to construct classes and compile methods. We modify the language tools so that they solely rely on the provided higher-level interface rather than being hardwired towards the low-level structural model used by the garbage collector. We show in various examples that by doing so we can easily implement new language abstractions and local customizations related to the state of objects.

Chapter 6 shows how first-class interpreters avoid having to build complex code transformations, or decompile low-level code, to modify the application semantics for language experimentation and debugging. We exemplify our approach by implementing three non-trivial debuggers.

Chapter 7 concludes the dissertation and outlines future work.

2
The Building Blocks of Object-Oriented Runtimes

In this chapter we shed light on the low-level implementation details of efficient object-oriented runtimes. We identify three fundamental building blocks used by the implementations, and explain how they impact performance.

Communication. Section 2.1 shows how efficient message sending is traditionally implemented.

Data. Section 2.2 explains the trade-offs of different run-time representations of objects. It discusses how objects are typically encoded at the lower level and how this influences the higher level.

Code. Section 2.3 focuses on different ways to encode and evaluate methods, and Section 2.4 explains the semantic operations performed by the code.

2.1 Communication: Efficient Message Dispatch

In procedural languages, functions are said to be *early-bound*, *i.e.*, they directly call each other. Dynamic object-oriented languages on the other hand support polymorphism through *late-bound* message sends. Rather than directly calling a function, message passing between objects is used to dynamically select which method is activated. Message dispatch is a central feature of object-oriented languages. For the language to be efficient, it is important that virtual message dispatch be fast. There is a myriad of techniques to implement efficient message dispatch. In this section we will discuss *lookup caches*, *virtual method tables*, *inline caches*, and *method inlining*.

2.1.1 Lookup Cache

In dynamically typed languages, the message is looked up in the message dictionaries of the inheritance hierarchy. To limit the lookup time, Smalltalk traditionally uses a global lookup cache (GLC) that maps the selector and class onto the related method [65, 89]. The size of the GLC is typically decided up front to limit memory usage. A GLC with 256 entries is reported to be effective about 90% of the time [89]. Alternatively lookup caches can be stored locally on a per-class basis.

While providing a more modest speedup than the following optimizations, lookup caches have the advantage that they can be used by purely interpretive implementations. All of the following optimizations are generally implemented in context of a statically compiled or JIT-compiled application for maximum performance.

2.1.2 Virtual Method Tables

In statically typed languages like Simula, C++, Java, *etc.*, objects that require virtual method dispatch traditionally contain a pointer to a *virtual method table* in their object header. Since types specify exactly what methods are supported by their implementors, the different methods can be numbered. Virtual method invocation is simply implemented by direct access of the virtual method table. This implementation method incurs two types of costs, a direct cost and an indirect cost [46]. The direct cost comes from having to select the right target procedure at runtime. The indirect cost stems from optimizations such as inlining that cannot be performed because the target of a call is unknown at compile time.

2.1.3 Inline Caches

Around 90% of sites where message are sent are *monomorphic* [41, 144, 27], *i.e.*, only have one receiver type. *Inline caching*, storing the method related to the expected type at the send site, drastically reduces the direct cost of message sending in natively compiled dynamic languages. Inline caching is implemented as follows. Initially a send site is *unlinked*. For example, the following Smalltalk message send:

```
bank accept: money
```

is typically compiled to the following pseudo native code:

```
load bank
load money
```

```
load #accept:
call invoke
```

The code first loads the receiver (bank), the arguments (money) and the selector (#accept:), and then calls to a meta-level invoke function which performs a full invocation sequence.

Message sends are *linked* as a side-effect of the invoke function. It stores the type of the receiver and the implementation of the message used during the invocation at the send site. Before a subsequent message send, the type of the new receiver is compared with the cached receiver type. If the type is the same, the cached method is directly reused. This avoids the cost of a full message lookup whenever the cache *hits*.

In the context of a GLC the cost of a message lookup is fairly minimal. The more significant overhead is due to the fact that the CPU executes instructions in a pipelined, out-of-order fashion: for higher performance, multiple instructions in a single sequence are handled in parallel[1]. Pipelined CPUs are best at handling calls to static targets. Since the code statically identifies the target, the CPU can up-front ensure that the target code is loaded in the instruction cache, and prefill the CPU pipeline with its code. Dynamic targets are partially supported using a *branch target buffer*, a specialized cache that stores the expected target for each location using a dynamic call. This allows the CPU to *speculatively* continue execution [25]. However, if all calls are dynamic, the branch target buffer quickly overflows, once more incurring large penalties due to pipeline stalls and instruction cache misses. Inline caches avoid this overhead by dynamically rewriting the code so that the cached method is the static target. In practice the call to invoke is replaced at run time by a direct call to the cached method. Instead of loading the selector, the cached type is loaded for type-checking. This transforms the previous code into:

```
load bank
load money
load Bank           // Instead of #accept:.
call Bank>>accept:  // Instead of invoke.
```

By directly calling the cached method, the CPU can properly prefetch its code.

To complement this implementation, all methods have a *preamble* that performs the required type-checking. If the type check fails, the preamble falls back to the invoke method to perform a full lookup. Since cached methods do not get the selector passed in anymore, methods store their own selector for falling back to invoke. A typical preamble looks as follows:

```
// Execute the method if receiver is of the expected type.
// The expected_type is passed in via the caller, bound to
// Bank by the code above.
```

---

[1]Parallel handling of instructions is only done where the CPU can prove there is no data dependency between the instructions.

```
    cmp type_of(receiver), expected_type
    je body
    // Otherwise, load the selector and fall back to invoke.
    load #accept:
    jmp invoke
body:
    ...
```

Because of the high cost of message lookup, the failing lookups may still take up a large amount of time. For example, by relying only on monomorphic inline caches, Self still spent up to 25% of its time handling inline cache misses [74]. *Polymorphic inline caches* further reduce overhead by caching multiple methods where a limited set of receiver types is expected [74]. In practice this causes the runtime system to allocate a short piece of executable memory in a buffer. Rather than calling to invoke or to a cached_method, the send site is modified to call to this buffer. The buffer itself contains code that branches based on already encountered types:

```
    cmp type_of(receiver), Bank
    je Bank>>accept:
    cmp type_of(receiver), Person
    je Person>>accept:
    ...
    load #accept:
    call invoke_extend_cache
```

Whenever a new type of receiver is encountered, the cache grows dynamically. However, when the number of encountered types exceeds a statically determined value, it is degenerated to a so-called *megamorphic* send site. The polymorphic inline cache is removed and replaced with an invoke that always performs a full lookup.

Since inline caches avoid the memory indirection of virtual method tables, and improve branch target prediction, they have shown to have competitive performance [47].

2.1.4 Method Inlining

Profile-guided receiver class prediction and *static class hierarchy analysis* further mitigate the direct and indirect cost of message dispatch [35, 67, 4]. A virtual method is compiled by merging all its statically found implementations into a single native function. At run-time a *class test* is performed to select the right implementation of the method within the function. This allows the static compiler to mitigate the indirect cost of virtual method dispatch by inlining the whole combined method, and optimizing every branch. It can further mitigate the direct cost of dispatch as well by inlining multiple methods that dispatch on the same receiver. Additionally it can result in improved performance by avoiding an indirect data access, avoiding potential data cache misses and resulting pipeline stalls.

Since in the previously described setup it is more cumbersome to support dynamic loading of code, other research replaced the class test with a *method test* [40]. Objects still refer to a virtual method table, and the call-site loads the address of the target method from the table. Rather than jumping to the retrieved address however, it is compared to the original address of the inlined code as guard for the inlined code. If the guard succeeds, the inlined code is directly executed. Otherwise the retrieved code is executed. This setup incurs the overhead of an extra load, but it ensures that code can easily be replaced at runtime while mitigating the cost of call-sites that remain unaffected by loaded code.

In dynamic runtimes, method inlining can still be performed by using runtime type feedback [75]. This type information is automatically collected in the context of PICs. Type feedback has been shown to compete with static type inference [3]. Dynamic method inlining is especially important for interactive systems that are extensible at run time.

2.1.5 Customization

While methods can be inherited in object-oriented languages, this has an adverse effect on optimization techniques. Since different subtypes may have usage patterns of inherited methods, the expected types may differ significantly. This reduces the effectiveness of optimization techniques.

Self relies on *customization* [29] to limit the scope, and thus increase the effectiveness, of inline caches and method inlining. Customization is the process of customizing a method towards an expected type. In particular, in Self all inherited methods are *copied down* to the inheriting clone family. By copying down methods the compiler statically knows the type of the receiver in every activation. This means that the target methods of messages sent to the receiver (self) are statically known, and thus can be inlined. Additionally, by copying down methods, dynamic lookups through multiple inherited message dictionaries are replaced by a single lookup in the dictionary containing all copied methods.

2.2 Data: Object Format and Management

The exact possible layouts of objects in memory is the *object format* supported by the programming language. The format definitions are mostly constrained by how memory is managed in the programming language, whether it be manually managed or automatically. In this section we shed light on the different constraints coming from the hardware, as well as from garbage collection techniques.

2.2.1 Hardware Constraints

Languages that let their users manage the memory of their programs often support highly customizable object formats. Since they do not need to provide optimized solutions for managing the memory they are more liberal in the object formats they support. The only rules imposed on the object format come from hardware and the OS for performance reasons. In this section we will introduce the most relevant hardware constraints.

Data structure alignment improves reading and writing speed since CPUs do not read out single bytes at a time [45]. For example, reading out a *word* that is not aligned requires reading out two separate words, masking out the relevant substructures and merging them together. Bigger structures are often aligned on larger boundaries since the CPU reads out multiple words at the same time[2]. To ensure data alignment compilers sometimes need to insert dummy elements into data structures, a technique called *data structure padding*. In C developers can take alignment into account by structuring their objects so that fields that require less space than a single alignment unit are grouped together, avoiding space overhead due to unnecessary padding, in turn reducing pressure on data caches.

Data cache locality is an important property that benefits from the insight a developer has in his own applications. Most modern CPUs rely on multi-level caching. The caches are divided into relatively small blocks (*e.g.*, 64 bytes), called *cache lines*. Memory is not loaded into the caches based on the exact size of used objects, but rather in the size of the cache lines. By moving related objects together, we increase the chance that the memory holding a subsequently accessed object is already *hot*, *i.e.*, will already be loaded into the data cache as a side-effect of a previously loaded object [45, 25]. In modern high-performance CPUs (and multi-core CPUs), cache misses dominate the execution cost since they are two to three orders of magnitude more expensive than the execution of single instructions [45, 25].

Unlike most high-level garbage collected languages, manually managed languages allow developers to inline objects into other objects. This does not only avoid unnecessary pointers, reducing the pressure on the data caches, but also ensures that the contained objects are close to their containers. This is most effective for arrays of a fixed type, increasing the speed of bulk operations for which cache locality is even more important.

Since memory allocation is fairly expensive, even in manually managed languages, systems languages often allow objects to be allocated on the stack directly. This eases memory reclamation since the data is automatically given back to the system when the frame in which the object was allocated is left. It also improves data cache locality since the stack is almost always hot.

Unfortunately, the performance of a manually memory-managed appli-

---

[2]Some instructions do not enforce data alignment but are just faster when their arguments are aligned. For this reason the Mac OS X ABI enforces 16-byte stack alignment on function calls by testing the alignment whenever the code jumps to system libraries.

cation is not always adequate since not all developers using systems programming languages have the knowledge required to structure their applications favorably: In practice, caches are under-exploited [26]. Another example of a common mistake is to declare independent global variables in the same context, while they are supposed to be used by different threads. If the compiler places the variables in the same data cache line, the resulting performance suffers due to *false sharing* [79, 25]: on each write to the variable in one thread, the cache line of the second thread needs to be updated via a slower cache, even though logically there is no need.

Another downside to the approach of letting developers handle their memory manually is that it often results in *memory leaks* (forgetting to free up unreferenced memory), *dangling pointers* (the use of pointers to already freed memory), *etc.*, that are difficult to debug [131]. While systems programming languages give the control to the user, there is a lack of adequate tools to detect such bugs. In either case, manual memory management is a very complex task that takes away a lot of time otherwise better spent on solving the problem at hand, but it is often desirable for memory- and performance-critical applications.

2.2.2 Garbage Collection Constraints

In a response to the previously described problems with manual memory management, many modern programming languages make use of a garbage collector.

Initially concerns were raised about the performance of automatic memory management. Nevertheless, similar to compilers obviating the need for hand-written assembler code, high-performance garbage collected runtimes automatically apply complex optimizations at run-time that are difficult to statically perform. For example, generational GCs are easily modified to optimize data cache locality [33]. Thread-local heaps can avoid false sharing in many cases [12]. Escape analysis has been used to relieve pressure from the GC by converting heap allocations into stack allocations, and by *scalar replacement*, avoiding object allocation by mapping their instance variables directly onto registers [28, 88]. However, since the user cannot declare his intent in the programming language directly, the GC is only left with reconstructing the assumptions through analysis.

The object format of garbage collected languages is imposed by their GC. It is designed for minimum GC code complexity, minimal allocation overhead, and maximum data cache locality. The number of paths through the GC code is decreased by limiting the number of object types. Allocation overhead is often avoided by using immediate values, *i.e.*, values that are not allocated on the heap. The cache locality is increased by directly storing structural meta-data required by the GC in the object header so that the class does not need to be loaded.

Immediate values. Most objects in garbage collected languages are allocated on the heap. They are passed around in the running program by reference, speeding up passing the object and ensuring consistency throughout the program. Nevertheless heap allocation is expensive.

This overhead can be reduced by encoding a limited set of data types, *e.g.*, integers, as immediate values. Because of data alignment used in most VMs, the references to objects do not vary in all bits of a pointer's value. In case of 32 bit (4 byte) or larger object alignment, the least significant two bits of the pointer are always zero. These bits are available to the language to encode (at least) three extra data types directly in the pointer, rather than allocating them on the heap. There are two requirements for data types to be suitable for immediate encoding: (1) the value needs to be immutable since it is passed by copying, and (2) the data type must fit in the bits remaining after applying the tag bits. Traditionally 32 bit Smalltalk systems encode small integers as signed 31 bit tagged pointers. Some VMs, such as the V8 JavaScript VM, also encode characters as immediate values. This is particularly useful when performing a lot of string operations. Floats are a third potential immediate value. All of these types of values can be encoded in the available space in a pointer minus the tag bits.

The downside of using tagged pointers is that it is asymmetric. All locations that dereference object pointers need to be aware that the pointer might actually be an encoded data type. Having to test for different object encodings introduces an overhead on standard operations. In case the code executes natively, more code space is required to test for the different cases. This overhead is offset by the speed increase by avoiding object allocation and by having direct access to the encoded value through the tagged pointer. The overhead is further reduced by applying static and dynamic optimizations that eliminate superfluous type guards.

A second criticism of tagged pointers is that they are not useful given that JIT compilation can perform the so-called *unboxing* of these values at runtime where required, without having to manually ensure it everywhere in the code. However, by solely relying on JIT compilation for unboxing, not all sites will run optimally (those that are not yet optimized), the JIT compiler has more work and will thus optimize the code slower, and startup is slower. The last point is especially crucial for short-lived scripts.

Object headers. Objects generally store meta-level information in an object extension known as the *object header*. The object header implies a memory overhead for objects, so is generally as small as possible. On the other hand, by storing meta-data directly in the object itself the language improves data cache locality and avoids indirections for object manipulation and garbage collection. Just like there is a wide variety of object encodings, there is a variety of object headers.

Dynamically typed object-oriented languages need at least a link from the object to type information that is used to look up methods at runtime. In class-based languages this link points to the class. Since a class pointer is required for inline caching, even highly optimized prototype-based languages rely on an internal class-like object to store behavior.

While garbage collected languages could look at the class to decide how to handle an instance, it is more efficient to get the meta-information directly from the object. For this purpose object headers often include multiple bits that are relevant to the GC, including the size and type of the object. The commonly used *mark-and-sweep* GC requires one bit per object to mark the object as being used. Reference counting garbage collectors on the other hand require more space to store the number of references to the object. In both cases the object header encodes the exact size of the object, and which segment of the object contains pointers to other objects.

Languages that frequently store objects in dictionaries require good dictionary performance. This is the case especially for languages using hash tables as native object representation, *e.g.*, Python. There are two basic operations on objects used to support dictionary access, hashing and equality. To improve the performance of dictionary access, objects often use a portion of the object header to store the *identity hash*.

2.3 Code: Method Structure

A layer of interpretation is often introduced between the CPU and the actual code. This provides language developers with a choice between different code formats. We give an overview of the most common formats: AST nodes, bytecodes, threaded code, and native code. We discuss the trade-offs between the different formats in terms of understandability, memory usage, and performance.

2.3.1 AST

The most high-level execution format that is widely used is the AST (abstract syntax tree) [81]. ASTs represent the essential structure of methods defining its behavior. After semantic analysis has been applied to match variable declarations and uses, they form a DAG (directed acyclic graph). Interpreters can walk the resulting DAG to evaluate the code. ASTs are very close to the original source of a program, making it an ideal format for interpretation and debugging. For ease of implementation, most interpreter prototypes rely solely on nested AST evaluation.

By representing AST nodes as objects, the interpreter can rely on polymorphism to evaluate the AST nodes by recursively descending the DAGs. This results in a very fine-grained call-stack that does not only keep track of activations, but also of the exact position within the AST. These call-stack operations are however superfluous since they dynamically keep track of state that is statically known. For example, suppose we are executing the following nested expression:

```
(a + b) * c
```

During execution the runtime will push the values related to a and b on the operand stack. Before sending the message +, however, it will need to remember that after returning, the message * needs to be sent. This is remembered by pushing the expression * c on a separate expression stack. This does not only imply direct execution overhead related to managing the expression stack, but also indirect overhead from additional cache and pipeline pressure.

The overhead of evaluating a nested AST can be reduced by flattening the DAG at compile-time in depth-first order. To keep track of the position within the resulting list of expressions it suffices to store the method or function and a single *program counter* for each activation. For extra performance, the counter can be mapped onto a register and only needs to be written back to the stack on activations. The disadvantage of flattening the AST is that the original nesting is not preserved. However, by storing extra meta-data in the nodes this structure can be recovered for debugging. Alternatively, a debugger can regenerate this information on-the-fly when required.

2.3.2 Bytecode

Even after flattening its DAG, the resulting AST still has a performance and memory downside. By encoding code in objects, the resulting AST uses more space than necessary for execution. Especially if the AST nodes are reified in the base-language, all AST nodes have an object header and use full pointers to link to their members. When no care is taken to allocate the AST nodes optimally by placing related AST nodes near each other, a single function might require several cache lines to be loaded, adding even more unnecessary data cache pressure.

Bytecode does not suffer from these problems since it is encoded minimally. They encode language-level operations using bytes, just like native code, but provide codes generally not offered by a general purpose CPU. This allows bytecodes to express language-level concepts more concisely than native code. An additional advantage over native code is that bytecodes are portable across multiple architectures. By writing an interpreter for bytecodes in a language supported by the required targets, the language can automatically be made available on all those platforms.

The evaluation of bytecodes is similar to that of flattened AST nodes. Since bytes are not objects, a bytecode interpreter is more complex than an AST evaluator. A bytecode interpreter relies on bit-masking and a multi-way branch (such as a *switch* statement or a *branch table*) to map the bytes onto their semantic operations. Rather than reading out operands from the expression objects, operands are decoded from the bytecodes or additional follow-up bytes. While expression objects can directly link to operand objects, bytes cannot easily directly encode other objects[3]. This is simplified by storing such objects close to the bytecode, for example in a literal frame or a constant pool, and using the operand as an index into this literal frame.

Direct bytecode interpretation is not particularly efficient [53]. Additionally it is criticized to be too far from the source code [42, 37]. This makes bytecodes a bad medium for understanding the source code. To understand the code, the bytecodes need to be decompiled or interpreted by an application. Debuggers that handle bytecodes rely on external meta-data to map the bytecodes back onto the original source code. For further dynamic optimizations it is most useful to have a high-level view on the source code, to understand and optimally encode the intent of the program. By using bytecodes as a source for optimizations, most of the intent is hidden between implementation details, making it harder to recover the original design. Nevertheless, given that without dynamic optimizations bytecodes can easily achieve higher performance than AST evaluation, bytecodes remain a more popular code format for more advanced interpreters.

2.3.3 Threaded Code

Profiling where AST evaluators and bytecode interpreters spend most of their time reveals that the main dispatch loop shows up high in the ranking. While the dispatch loop is a very simple piece of code that only chooses how to evaluate instructions, the CPU has to return to it before each instruction. The code then jumps to the implementation of the actual next opcode implementation. This implies two branches for each evaluated instruction: an indirect branch (computed jump to the return address on the stack) from the previous instruction back to the dispatch loop, and a conditional branch from the dispatch loop to the next instruction. Since all conditional branches occur in the same dispatch loop, the branch target predictor of the CPU cannot possibly properly predict the branch taken, resulting in costly pipeline stalls between instructions.

To minimize the overhead, other types of *virtual machine instruction sets* are used. Threaded code[4] [9] removes the need for a centralized dispatch loop by directly storing the target interpreter function addresses in sequence as the main code representation. Whenever an instruction finishes evaluation it can directly jump to the next instruction without having to first return to a main dispatch loop. Threaded code improves performance over bytecode interpretation, further closing the performance gap between interpretation and native code compilation. Threaded code is however easier to port across platforms than complete native code compilers. Since there is a one-to-one mapping between both formats, it is easy to generate equivalent threaded code on-the-fly while loading bytecode.

---

[3] By mixing bytecodes with object pointers the resulting methods become harder to garbage collect, resulting in performance overhead. The garbage collector would require knowledge of all bytecodes to find references to other objects.

[4] Note that threaded code in this context is unrelated to *multi-threading*.

There are two main threaded code encodings that are of interest:

Direct-threaded code contains machine addresses in a thread of code, *i.e.*, a simple array of code pointers. During execution the runtime keeps track of the current location within the thread using pointer that represents the program counter. Interpretation is started by jumping to the value at the initial program counter. Whenever an instruction finishes it increases the program counter and direct jumps to its value without further need for decoding. The program counter namely points at the address of the implementation of the next instruction.

The following code implements a push_true instruction:

```
push_true:
    stack_push(true);
    goto **(pc += 1);
```

The code is labeled so that can be used as jump target. The operand to be pushed on the stack is decoded from the thread by reading out the value directly following the current program counter. At the end the instruction directly jumps to the next instruction by increasing the program counter and jumping to its value, the address of the next instruction.

A problem with this code style is that the CPU cannot properly predict where the code wants to go next [54]. Suppose in a specific thread push_true is followed by push_false:

```
void* thread[] = { ...,
    &&push_true,
    &&push_false,
    ... };
```

Since the CPU sees goto **(pc += 1) rather than goto push_false, it cannot properly prefetch the instruction code. It has to wait until the target address at **(pc += 1) is available before it can load the code into the pipeline. While the branch target predictor normally helps by guessing the target based on previous executions, the multitude of opcode combinations occurring over all threads generally trashes this cache.

As the example shows, direct-threaded code requires being able to refer to native code fragments as jump targets. This is problematic [116, 53] since ANSI-C does not support *computed jump* (*indirect branch*) needed to jump to dynamically provided addresses. Most C implementations, *e.g.*, GNU C, do however provided a version of computed jump.

Context threaded code (*subroutine threaded code*) relies on generated native code to sequence interpreter operations [13]. Rather than just using pointers to the fragments that encode the semantics of instructions, subroutine threading relies on sequences of native calls to instruction functions. The following code implements push_true as context threaded instruction:

```
void push_true()
{
    stack_push(true);
}
```

The previous thread is encoded as:

```
void thread()
{   ...
    push_true();
    push_false();
    ...
}
```

This reintroduces the overhead of having single call-and-return sequences per instruction, but it avoids the overhead of not knowing what the next instruction is. Since the CPU directly executes the thread itself, thanks to the *return stack buffer*[5] it can pre-fetch the code related to next instruction, avoiding pipeline stalls.

The difficulty of subroutine threading is that native code needs to be generated and placed in executable memory. Rather than having full control over the execution in an interpreter, the runtime has to cooperate with the hardware to manage execution.

Because of the trade-offs involved, it depends on the hardware which of both previously described techniques is faster. Both, however, result in faster execution than vanilla bytecode execution.

Since threaded code uses full pointers to link to opcodes rather than single bytes, many more operations can directly be supported than in bytecode sets. To further increase the time spent doing useful work, superinstructions optimize threaded code by combining opcodes into larger single opcodes [116, 56]. Superinstructions reduce the need for reading and dispatch opcodes. If the superinstructions are generated at compile-time, the compiler can apply optimizations across opcodes that would otherwise be impossible. Useful combinations can be detected using static analysis of existing applications. Superinstructions reduce the size of threaded code, and decrease the required number of dispatches and resulting branch mispredictions [55]. Nevertheless they require more memory for native code, increasing pressure on the instruction cache.

---

[5]The CPU relies on a return stack buffer since return addresses are mutable on the native stack. The buffer is used as specialized branch target predictor. The CPU cannot be certain that push_true does not modify the return address to jump somewhere else than returning to thread (and subsequently call push_false).

The approach of relying on static analysis might however not fit applications that are dynamically loaded on top of the VM. For this reason, another approach [116] detects used opcode sequences at runtime. By statically meta-describing the implementations of primitive opcode fragments they can be copied and combined in a cache for superinstructions at runtime.

A difficulty in implementing direct-threaded interpreters in a higher-level language like C is that C compilers are designed to optimize normal user applications. The instructions of threading interpreters are implemented at a higher granularity than functions, using only fragments of functions. C compilers generally expect to optimize full functions as one block, which does not generete the optimal code for threaded instruction implementations. While not very portable across compiler versions, BrouHaHa [104] instead relies on specifically generated code by manually annotating variables with register names [105]. The newer LuaJIT interpreter [113] relies on handwritten assembler code for optimal performance.

2.3.4 Native Code

The previously defined code formats can limit themselves to operations that are first-class in the language. All required meta-level actions, *e.g.*, setting up a stack frame for activation, are implicit in the base-level operations. Since there is generally a mismatch between the language and the target hardware, compiling complex application-level operations fully to native code requires additional support code to be generated. For example to compile Smalltalk bytecodes to native X86 or X86-64 assembler, bytecodes are translated into one of the following three native code types:

- a single native instruction, like memory access or copying a register (accounts for ca. 175 Smalltalk-80 bytecodes),
- an expanded assembler template (their function is similar to CPU microcode, *e.g.*, copying a memory range),
- a function call (*e.g.*, opcodes that send messages).

The last case is used for code that is too expansive to inline. Instead the code calls to a meta-level library function that implements the required operation. Code that supports a programming language is provided in a so-called *runtime library*.

2.4 Code: Method Behavior

During execution a so-called *continuation* keeps track of the run-time state within the used code format. There are two sides to a continuation: the *runtime stack* and the *environment*. The runtime stack is split up into the *control state* and the *operand stack*. The control state captures the function-call nesting and the state within these functions. The operand stack contains the values required to evaluate expressions, and values resulting from evaluating expressions. The environment captures the data involved in activations: local variables, receiver and arguments.

2.4.1 Recursive interpretation

AST interpreters are easily written at a high level using the *interpreter pattern* or *visitor pattern*. The interpreter recursively visits code while manually managing the environments. The host language, rather than the interpreter itself, keeps track of the runtime stack. The environment is represented as heap-allocating environment frames that link to the return frame, and the lexical outer frame to support lambdas.

There are multiple disadvantages to the recursive approach however. Firstly by letting the host-language manage the recursion, the number of features easily provided to the base-language is limited to the set of stack-operations provided by the host-language. Secondly, by intertwining base-level recursion with meta-level recursion the stack frames used for base-level recursion will be larger than required since also the meta-level state is stored in each frame. This state is irrelevant, however, since it can be reconstructed fully from the state of the application alone. For example, suppose the following interpreter method evaluates an array of statements and returns the result of evaluating the last statement:

```
visitStatements: statements
    ↑ 1 to: statements size do: [ :pc |
        (statements at: pc) accept: self ]
```

The only data essential to keep track of evaluation are the `statements` array and the index into the array (`pc`). Nevertheless, the language in which the interpreter is written also keeps track of the state of the interpreter. This information is superfluous since there is only one possible position between statement evaluations: at the end of the `to:do:` loop.

2.4.2 Manual stack management

To get full control over the run-time state of an application the stack can be manually managed. Within a single method the state is explicitly represented by a *program counter*. Calls and returns require storing and restoring of this program counter. If this strategy is used on top of another language, the final runtime has two runtime stacks: one for the interpreter and one for the application. The interpreter itself is generally implemented as a loop that evaluates application-level code and does not require much stack space. The application stack will only contain the state required for the evaluation of the application and is therefore minimal.

As an alternative stack design the environment and the operand stack can be embedded into a single context frame that is wired in sequence to form the runtime stack. The advantage of embedding stack and environment is that it gives a first-class representation of the runtime state of an activation. Additionally, it is easy to reorganize the stack at runtime to implement language extensions that are otherwise hard to accomplish. Backtracking has been implemented on top of Smalltalk as an example use of first-class context objects [90].

2.4.3 Stack-mapped context frame

The downside of all the above approaches is that the context objects are allocated on the heap. Since activations happen at a much higher rate than any other activity in VMs, this accounts for a large percentage of object allocations and gives a large overhead to the garbage collector. Additionally, since these objects are heap-allocated they likely belong to different cache lines, causing extra strain on the CPU's memory management unit between method activations. This has a major impact on the performance of the runtime.

A first solution to this problem is to fix the size of context objects and cache them [89]. This avoids overhead in the garbage collector since they can be explicitly freed on return. In case a context object is captured by a closure it cannot be freed. Nevertheless the fixed size of the objects ensures it will not fragment the cache. However, captured contexts do separate logically consecutive calling contexts, increasing the risk of data cache misses. Additionally, every activation requires the runtime to write a back-pointer to the return context into the new context frame.

The overhead is alleviated by allocating the activation frames directly on a stack [106]. Frames are allocated by increasing the stack pointer, and are removed by decreasing the stack pointer. This wires stack frames together in the order of activations, ensuring that the related memory is most likely already loaded in the data cache. It however brings with it three difficulties:

Firstly, implementing closures is harder in a stack-mapped setup than in the others. Since context objects are not regular objects but part of a stack, they automatically disappear and potentially get overwritten when the method or closure is left. Values that are captured by a closure and have to live on beyond the life-span of the original activation would get lost. Simple static analysis of code can identify exactly which values need to be kept alive beyond the life-span of a stack frame. These values are stored in a separate, heap-allocated, *remote array*. By sharing the array between a context and the closures that capture it, the values are also shared, and can live on even though the frame they originated from has already terminated.

The second disadvantage is that stack frames are not as flexible as context objects, since they are implicitly sequenced. To support the same features as separately heap-allocated context objects, a lot of extra administration has to be performed. However, since most base-level code relies on regular activations it makes sense to improve performance in favor of regular use.

A final disadvantage is that a pre-allocated stack can overflow on deep recursion. This is solved in some approaches by not just implementing the stack as a single large chunk of memory, but rather a series of stack pages. On every activation the runtime checks if there is still space within the current stack page, and if not, it uses a next stack page to allocate the frame. The first stack frame of a stack page contains a pointer to *trampoline code, i.e.*, meta-level code that overcomes the limitation that the CPU expects the stack frames to be laid out in sequence. The trampoline code restores the previous stack page and returns to the top stack frame on that page. This setup avoids stack overflows, and is still faster than allocating separate context frames since it is more coarse-grained. Alternatively the virtual memory manager's page protection can be used to dynamically allocate extra stack pages or free unused pages. In that case the page protection traps are used as hardware-supported trampolines.

2.4.4 Register-Based Execution

Just like in hardware, there are two main execution models in software for handling operands: stack-based and register-based. The model used by a language does not necessarily directly relate to the model used by hardware. On the contrary, many languages such as Java and Smalltalk rely on a stack-based bytecode-set, while being available for register-based processors such as the X86.

Stack-based bytecode has the advantage of being smaller than register-based bytecode since often the operands are passed implicitly, relative to the stack pointer. In register-based languages the code always has to specify which variables are used in the operation. Register-based bytecode was found to be 26% larger than the equivalent [132].

Register-based bytecode has the advantage that it is not bound to a stack-based view of its application. This implies for example that superfluous values never need to be popped from the stack. Since there are fewer codes to be executed the final execution time is lower than for the stack-based alternative, in part due to the overhead of dispatching bytecodes [132].

2.5 Summary

We have identified three main building blocks of object-oriented languages:

- Message sending as communication between objects,
- the object encoding that declares how objects are laid out in memory, and how they are managed,
- method structure and behavior that encode the semantics of single methods.

We have explained the differences between the major design choices for all building blocks and how they impact performance. In the next chapter we will talk about how current approaches allow the user to hook into the defined building blocks, and the limitations thereof.

3
Background and Problems

In this chapter we discuss two main approaches that are targeted at making runtimes reusable. They form the basis of the related work we build upon. In Section 3.1 we give an introduction to run-time reflection, an approach that is designed to give applications the illusion that they have direct access to their own meta-level from within their runtime. In Section 3.2 we provide insights in the alternative approach of generating high-performance VMs from meta-circular implementations to streamline the development of new interpreters. The differences between our work and the related work are presented inline in the relevant chapters (Section 4.5, Section 5.7, and Section 6.5).

3.1 Reflection

Computational reflection refers to the ability of computer programs to reason about their own structure and behavior at runtime [134, 95]. Reflective systems distinguish the *base* (application) level from the *meta* (semantic) level. Reflection entails the *reification* of meta-level entities to the base level, that is, semantic entities are reified as ordinary application entities. (If we ask a Java object for its class, we obtain an ordinary Java object representing that class.)

Structural reflection is concerned with reification of the structure of the program, *i.e.*, its data and code. *Behavioral reflection* is concerned with reification of the behavior of the program, *i.e.*, its *interpretation*. Reflection can be further refined into *introspection* and *intercession*. Introspection is purely concerned with reifying meta-level concepts to reason about them at the base level. For example, we may ask an object what fields it has so we can print them all. Intercession, on the other hand, allows us to manipulate reified meta-level entities and *reflect* changes back to the meta-level. In Smalltalk, one can change the class of an object at runtime, immediately causing that object's behavior to change. Such changes effect a *causal connection* between the reified entities and the meta-level entities they represent [95].

Some typical uses of reflection are found in (i) debugging tools; (ii) GUIs for object structures; (iii) code instrumentation and analysis tools; (iv) dynamic code generation; and (v) language extensions. Several different approaches to behavioral reflection have been realized over the years.

Smith introduced the notion of computational reflection and he illustrated his model through the implementation of a reflective dialect of Lisp, called 3-Lisp [134]. 3-Lisp applications can contain special *reifier* functions that take reifications of aspects of the interpreter as arguments: the current expression, the environment in which the expression is being executed and the continuation of the application. In Smith's model these reifiers conceptually run in the scope of the interpreter since they operate on the application from the point of view of the interpreter. Adding support for reifiers to a language thus adds the ability to *add lines* to the code of the interpreter from within the application context. It also creates the illusion that below every interpreter, there is another interpreter that evaluates the interpreter and all reifications requested by the application on top. Reflection is therefore supported by an infinite *tower of interpreters*.

3.1.1 Discrete and Continuous Behavioral Reflection

Behavioral reflection in most systems is *discrete*, which means that reflective computations are initiated at a discrete point by calling a reflective procedure and only lasting until this procedure returns [98]. For example, a method wrapper that makes a method asynchronous only affects the particular wrapped method, not all the methods in the whole system.

Continuous behavioral reflection refers to reflective computations that modify existing structures of the meta-interpreters, thus having a continuous effect on the base level computation [98]. Software transactional memory, for example, entails a continuous change to the semantics of a language which can benefit from invasive changes to the runtime [69].

Smith's "tower of interpreters" approach is fundamentally discrete since the behavior of interpreters can only be extended, not modified. Existing meta-behavior cannot be mutated, strictly limiting custom reflective behavior to the base-level code explicitly triggering this custom reflective behavior. Simmons *et al.* extended the discrete reflective tower to a continuous model of reflection by introducing *first-class interpreters* in Refci (reflective extension by first-class interpreters) [133]. In Refci, changes can be applied to the interpreter by explicitly wrapping around the meta-interpreter. These wrappers are then used to interpret of all code to which the modified interpreter is applied, thus having a continuous effect on its interpretation.

Refci extends the interface of reifiers with reifications of the interpreter itself in the form of a *dispatch* procedure and *preliminary* procedures. The dispatch procedure evaluates expressions by selecting the right interpreter-level procedures. There is a single default dispatch that provides support for constants, identifiers, applications and special forms, and bad form errors. Since the dispatch handles all expressions, it is a reification of the actual interpreter. To extend the interpreter, a user writes a preliminary procedure. Preliminary procedures create a new dispatch from an existing one. They transform the dispatch to add support for new expressions, or to wrap around existing expression handlers, supporting modifications to the existing interpreter functionality. (We explain the similarities and differences between Refci and our approach in subsection 6.5.1.)

3.1.2 Separation of base and meta-level

Typically, discrete reflection is implemented by manipulating base-level code (*e.g.*, through source or bytecode transformation). This technique raises a whole new set of problems (the same that optimizers introduce for debugging). Most importantly, the application that uses reflection has to keep track of the meta-level on which it is being evaluated to avoid endless recursion [32, 38]. For instance, the code that logs a method execution must avoid itself triggering the logging meta behavior to avoid infinite meta recursion. This problem arises from the lack of a clean separation between base and meta behavior.

While towers of interpreters clearly separate the base-level and meta-level computations, metaobject protocols generally lack this clear distinction, leading to confusion between the two levels [32, 38].

At the same time, by conflating the reflective API of objects with their base-level API, it becomes impossible to guarantee proper encapsulation. McAffer [99] argues that "The implementation of an object must be explicitly exposed and clearly distinguished from the object's domain-specific behaviour description." Bracha and Ungar argue that "meta-level facilities must be separated from base-level functionality" [23]. They provide *mirrors*, objects acting as reflective proxies separate from the base-level objects they reflect upon.

3.1.3 Partial Behavioral Reflection

During a workshop on reflection, Smith mentioned that in the wide spectrum of reflective applications most applications only need a fragment of the information that can be provided by the interpreter [77]. Since reification of information is expensive due to wrapping into special objects, partial behavioral reflection tries to limit the number of reified objects and message sends needed during the execution of a program.

Partial behavioral reflection provides a reflective model that enables local extensions to the code by attaching metaobjects to operations through links. A link conditionally lets the metaobject decide about the evaluation of the operation that activated the link [141]. In the original model links are installed in the code at class-loading time. Unanticipated partial behavioral reflection extends the model by allowing dynamic installation and retraction of links [127]. The model was also further refined to hook into the high-level AST representations of the code rather than low-level bytecodes [36].

3.1.4 High-level reflective API

Reflection enabled by mechanisms such as method wrappers [24], proxies [48], or overriding exception handling methods [48] is used in practice only in limited, idiomatic ways depending on the host programming language. To enable widespread use of reflection, a safe and practical reflective API is needed.

Bracha and Ungar claim as a fundamental design principle for reflection that *"meta-level facilities must encapsulate their implementation"* [23]. McAffer justifies this principle as follows:

> the metalevel has been thought of as a place for making small changes requiring small amounts of code and interaction. We believe that the metalevel should be viewed as any other potentially large and complex application — it is in great need of management mechanisms. [100]

In an effort to make it feasible to develop libraries and applications that rely on reflection, Kiczales *et al.* proposed the use of *metaobject protocols* (MOPs) to implement discrete reflection.

> What reflection on its own doesn't provide, however, is flexibility, incrementality, or ease of use. This is where object-oriented techniques come into their own [85].

Since its definition, all reflective object-oriented languages have resorted to metaobject protocols to provide discrete reflection. By providing a clear interface to the language, metaobject protocols give the user the ability to incrementally customize the behavior and implementation of the language. Metaobject protocols provide discrete reflection since it requires installing custom metaobjects wherever non-standard behavior is required.

Open implementations [84] are a general design principle that moves the black box boundary of objects so that part of their internal implementation strategy becomes open and customizable to the user. For example a Set class could allow the user to specify what kind of operations are most common for a particular instance so that that instance can be optimized towards that use-case. Open implementations provide discrete customizations, affecting only particular instances rather than the system as a whole.

3.1.5 AOP

Aspect-Oriented Programming (AOP) [86] provides a domain-specific language for meta- and reflective programming [126]. It is designed specifically to target modularization of crosscutting concerns. It consists of two main parts, a set of *advices* that change the behavior of programs and a *pointcut language* that declaratively defines where the aspect system has to *weave* in the advices. Given that AOP is a language for reflection, it can be implemented by providing a pointcut language as a declarative front-end to reflection [136].

The power of AOP mainly comes from the pointcut language that makes the way shadow points are selected for local modifications easier and more understandable by being declarative.

Both partial behavioral reflection and AOP essentially apply structural intercession to the base-level code: they do not alter the evaluation of the base-level code but rather change the code to incorporate the new behavior. The developers of AspectJ even take pains to distinguish the implementation of AspectJ from classical computational reflection [86].

3.2 Generating Tailored Virtual Machines

In addition to compiling languages to existing VMs, as described in Chapter 1, VMs themselves are increasingly built to be adaptable at compile-time. The idea of generating high-performance VMs from meta-circular definitions has been explored to a greater extent in several projects [78, 80, 143, 19]. This approach does not only require building a high-level meta-circular VM but also a compiler toolchain that can optimize the VM to be at least as fast as (and potentially faster than) a manually written interpreter. The difference in the various projects lies in the language being implemented by the VM, and more importantly, the expressiveness of the actual subset of the language used in the definition of the meta-circular VM.

The Squeak VM [78] is written in a Smalltalk dialect called Slang. The dialect is a severely limited subset of Smalltalk that eases compilation to C. Polymorphic message sends are compiled away to early-bound function calls. Certain operations have two distinct implementations, one for running in emulation mode on top of another interpreter, and another for after translation.

The Jikes RVM [80], a meta-circular Java VM, bootstraps from a minimal image that is cross-compiled from a pre-existing JVM, and then loaded by a small C program. From there on, all VM services are provided by code written in plain Java that operates at the same level as other Java code. All Java bytecode is compiled to native code using virtual method tables.

In the Klein project [143] a metacircular virtual machine is implemented for the Self language [142]. The Klein VM is written in Self and follows object-orientation, metacircularity and code reuse. Klein hardwires the object model of Self objects. Klein objects are described by *maps*, objects that describe the behavior of objects. To break infinite meta-recursion, Klein hardwires a single *map of maps*. Klein bootstraps by cross-compiling a bootstrapping image, using the dynamic compilation infrastructure that compiles Self code to native code. The bootstrap image is cloned from a subset of the Self objects in an already running development Self VM, written in C++. Some of the required meta-level code, the clone method and message lookup (in case of inline cache miss), is written in an extremely low-level, message-free, variant of the Self language. The bootstrap image can be a self-contained Self application, or contain a Self interpreter. For ease of VM development, the bootstrap image is sent to a debug server (written in C(++)) that starts the new Klein VM in a separate process. After booting the new VM, the development VM can reflectively inspect and modify objects in the remote VM, using mirror-based reflection [23] supported by the debug server.

PyPy [123] follows a similar approach to the Squeak VM, although it is written in a more expressive subset of the Python language, called RPython. PyPy interpreters are developed as a high-level model, scripted together at load time using the full Python language. Once an interpreter is fully loaded in the Python runtime, type inference is applied, and a garbage collector and a JIT compiler are woven in. The toolchain then specializes the resulting code to a back-end, *e.g.*, C, which is subsequently translated to native code. Since RPython is more expressive than Slang, it is more attractive for other language implementations, *e.g.*, Squeak [18].

3.3 Problem 1: The Tyranny of a Closed VM

VMs provide a higher-level interface to the actual target machines. It provides an intermediate language, most often in the form of bytecodes, that is targeted by compiler builders of higher-level languages. This facilitates implementing programming languages since compiler builders only have to go half-way. Nevertheless there are several problems with using a pre-compiled VM.

VMs are closed for extension. The Common Language Runtime is a VM for a whole family of languages [102]. It shows how a unified infrastructure can ease the development and maintenance of language implementations. Nevertheless, a single VM cannot anticipate all needs of languages it was not initially designed to support. For example, the JVM initially did not support dynamic method invocations. Unfortunately, VMs are classically black boxes: they define fixed interfaces (*i.e.*, bytecode and an API) for accessing the features they provide. To extend a VM, one must open the black box, and define a custom adaptation. Custom VMs, however, introduce branches in the VM implementation, sacrificing compatibility and risking rapid obsolescence. Additionally, users are forced to choose between features added by different custom VMs, or they have to combine them into yet another custom VM. Examples of now incompatible VMs include the object-flow VM [93] built as an extension to Squeak, and Iguana/J [120] which introduced fine-grained MOP extensions to the JVM.

Host language bias or lock-in. VMs are usually tailored towards the language for which they were initially developed. Since the JVM is built for Java, an object-oriented language, it lacks features required by other languages that target it. To support languages from the LISP family for example, tail call elimination needs to be implemented. Since this feature is not available in the JVM, Clojure [72] does not try to work around this limitation but instead introduces an explicit new language feature that implements iteration. The main problem is that language developers cannot reuse parts of the VM and replace others with their own code.

Reflection and meta programming restrictions. A VM implements the meta-level behavior of a programming language. As a consequence, support for reflection and metaprogramming must be provided by a MOP. Reflective extensions to the VM need to be supported up-front. For example, to allow arbitrary objects to be treated like regular method dictionaries, VMs generally include manually written tests:

```
if (method_dictionary.class == MethodDictionary) {
    Dictionary_at(method_dictionary, selector);
} else {
    send(method_dictionary, "at:", selector);
}
```

The code checks whether the method dictionary is of the type known to the VM. If it is, the method dictionary is directly accessed. If it is another type of object however, the VM invokes the method at: on the object, passing the selector as argument. This approach is inconsistent with the polymorphic behavior normally exhibited by the language [32]. Rather than sending a polymorphic message, the VM developer needs to manually insert these extension points wherever he sees fit. After compilation, the extension points are hard-wired into the runtime and inaccessible. It is not possible for a user to introduce unforeseen reflective capabilities to the system. Many Smalltalk VMs provide reflective access to the method dictionaries in classes, but do not support custom method dictionaries at runtime. Those VMs crash when an instance of a customized class receives a message, since they violate the encapsulation of the meta-level object by grabbing the method directly out of the dictionary's memory.

Douance *et al.* [44] claim that it is useful to build custom interpreters that embed new reflective capabilities in an effort to optimize the amount of information that is actually reified. They propose to implement specific changes by modifying a meta-circular interpreter that is compiled to a new interpreter for each specific metaobject protocol.

Language interoperability issues. Interoperability is a key requirement for the evolution of a language. Even though we might not care about interoperating with other languages, it is vital that new versions of a language will be able to interact with older versions of the same language.

While many modern programming languages are only slight variations in semantics of one another (especially in the case of different versions of the same language), they are generally not compatible in terms of libraries, runtimes and tools. To run a second language in a runtime, the second language needs to adapt as well as possible to the first for performance and interoperability. Even if the second language has a better performance potential than the first, it is rather difficult for the second to surpass the performance of the first. Feature sharing between both languages is often problematic because of mismatches in object model and execution semantics. If a third language is implemented on top of the first language, interoperability between the second and third language is even less guaranteed to work out of the box.

3.4 Problem 2: Low-level Object Structure

Once we zoom in on individual garbage collected objects, we see that the object models are necessarily hardwired in the GC. For performance reasons, a GC generally only supports a single type of object format. Garbage collected languages handle this by defining one specific object model that can be supported by their GC. These languages, however, do not build further upon this most basic object model, but use it throughout the language as only object representation. As a result the expressiveness, as well as the performance of the language, suffer. While manually managed languages provide a higher degree of control over the final data layout, garbage collected languages only provide few hardwired choices. The main customization features that remain in statically typed languages are the static types, and potentially a limited set of *primitive data types*. We divide dynamic languages into two categories based on their encoding of objects:

Objects as arrays. In languages like Smalltalk-80, objects are references to arrays of objects, raw bytes, or words, or they are immediately encoded as *tagged pointers*. By representing objects as references to arrays, a minimal amount of space is used, and member access is highly optimized.

As a downside, code has to know up-front which array indices correspond to which members, and exactly how many members will be stored in the object. In this scheme, dynamic changes to the layout of objects are expensive since they require extensive changes throughout the whole application. Finally, external meta-data is required to understand the semantics of an object since by itself it is just an array of pointers.

Objects as hash-tables. The objects in Python, JavaScript, Ruby, *etc.*, can grow dynamically based on the code that operates on them. Conceptually, these languages encode their objects as hash-tables. The advantage of dynamically growing objects is that it becomes easier to dynamically load new code that use such additional slots. By storing fields as key-value pairs it is easy to inspect and understand objects at runtime.

Runtime extensible objects pose an extra hurdle for optimizations. VMs like the V8 JavaScript engine require tricks to mitigate the overhead by transparently transforming the object format back to a Smalltalk-80-style object format. This way slot lookup can be converted to simple array accesses rather than dictionary lookups.

Garbage collected languages solely providing hash tables as a flexible object model have a hard time optimizing this model in terms of memory usage and runtime performance. On the other hand, languages that provide an array-based object model do not easily support dynamic extensions. In both cases, there is only focus on how to store the data, not how it is initialized and accessed at run-time. The language makes trade-offs about the storage for its users and does not allow developers to decide by themselves what object encoding is useful at any given time.

3.5 Problem 3: Low-Level Execution Model

Meta-tools such as debuggers, profilers, and sandboxing need to continuously reflect on the behavior of applications. Just like the construction of VMs, building debuggers and profiles is a tedious task mostly left to experts resulting in generic tools. These resulting tools are only rarely customizable by the user to fit his needs in a particular situation. The need for custom tools is clear however, given that most developers reach out to lower level and less scalable, but more customizable means like print statements.

Building such tools is difficult because the executable format of programming language code is expressed in terms of the low-level execution engine. The problem is that there is a large gap between the low-level execution model and the mental model a programmer has of his application. Debuggers are often specified in terms of the low-level model since they are the only representation of the application available at run-time. While meta-information about the executable code is sometimes available, this is generally not an executable model, preventing light-weight semantics modifications.

3.6 Summary

We have presented a short overview of the implementation of programming languages

In this chapter, we have discussed work related to opening up language runtimes to fundamental changes. We have focused on reflection as a technique to change a runtime from within, and the technique of generating high-performance VMs from higher-level models as a technique to lower the cost of building runtimes tailored to the requirements of a language. From there on we have identified three problems resulting from limitations of existing reflective models and of VMs:

1. VMs are hardwired towards a particular language or language family, and do not support fundamental modifications at run-time.

2. Languages only support a single set of predefined encodings of objects.

3. The gap between run-time code and source code limits the development of debuggers and profiles.

In the following chapters we tackle these problems one by one. Chapter 4 enforces polymorphism at the meta-level by implementing a self-supporting runtime library. Chapter 5 extends the structural model of the language with first-class support for object layouts, enabling user-defined layout customizations. Chapter 6 introduces first-class AST interpreters as basis for continuous behavioral reflection.

4
First-Class Message Lookup

It has been argued that a VM should be built using the techniques and patterns that are established in normal software engineering [99, 143]. We argue that this principle should not only hold for the implementation of the language runtime, but also for the behavior of a compiled and running system. Similar to the introduction of field programmable gate arrays, we argue that a VM should not be a hardwired black box with bytecode as arbitrary cutoff level. Instead it should be a combination of a standardized interface to all components, a reusable runtime library to support the used language.

In this chapter we efficiently reify the most basic building block of object-oriented languages: the communication between objects by sending messages. The presented model standardizes the interface between objects, and supports custom message handling semantics on a per-object basis. This is the most basic building block since it allows developers to freely choose language semantics at object boundaries.

Pinocchio provides messaging semantics as a self-supporting runtime library. The runtime library replaces the traditional VM by implementing meta-level semantics, like message sending, directly in Smalltalk. Since the runtime library is itself implemented in Smalltalk *and* is first-class, it also serves as its own runtime library. It is therefore inherently self-supporting.

Objects and code from the base- and meta-level are therefore unified. They can flow between the two, and base-level objects can polymorphically replace meta-level objects. Thus all parts of the runtime library are composed of run-time accessible and reusable parts. Since the runtime library implements the behavior of the Smalltalk language, behavioral reflection is available to the language as a side-effect of the uniformity of the system.

We will provide several examples illustrating how extensions to the runtime can be achieved by replacing part of the meta-level at run time. In particular we show how the Pinocchio runtime can be adapted to support prototype-based message lookup.

The contributions of this chapter are:

- we propose a novel approach to realizing a truly self-supporting runtime that does not rely on interpretation or bytecode;

- we demonstrate how a formal unification of meta- and base-level code enables runtime extensions;

- we present evidence that a self-supporting and extensible runtime can be implemented efficiently; and

- we demonstrate that typical language extensions in such a runtime can be realized with modest effort.

Outline We provide a high-level overview of our approach in Section 4.1. In Section 4.2 we describe the key elements of the design and implementation of the self-supporting, extensible Pinocchio language runtime. We provide a series of examples of typical extensions in Section 4.3, and show how they can be easily achieved in Pinocchio by substituting meta-level objects with compatible run-time[1] objects. In Section 4.4 we review several of the perceived benefits of VM-based approaches to the implementation of languages, and discuss how these points are impacted by the approach. We discuss related work in Section 4.5 and summarize the chapter in Section 4.6.

4.1 The Message is the Medium

In the previous chapter we have seen that a conventional VM is a closed black box, offering only a restricted MOP to support reflection and metaprogramming (see left side of Figure 4.1). The implementation of the VM is compiled away, and is not accessible to the running application, except through the pre-defined MOP. Extensions required to support new programming languages can be achieved only by constructing a custom VM, negatively impacting reusability and compatibility.

In contrast, the Pinocchio runtime consists of objects sending messages. The semantics of receiving messages is defined by object-specific meta-levels. These meta-levels are, just like application code, implemented using objects and messages. The entire Pinocchio runtime is accessible to application code, rather than just a restricted MOP. Furthermore, to realize extensions, Pinocchio's meta-level objects can be replaced at run time by compatible application objects (see Figure 4.1, right side).

---

[1] The Pinocchio *runtime* enables *run-time* extensions, *i.e.*, at *run time* as opposed to compile time.

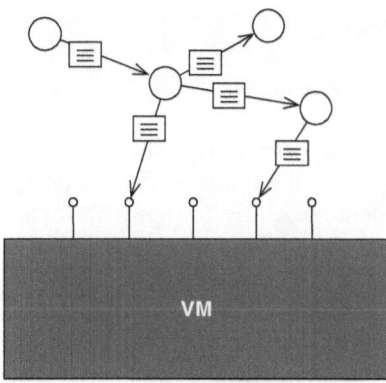 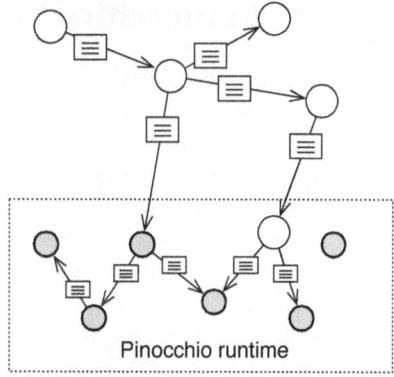

Figure 4.1: A conventional VM (left) is closed, offering only a fixed API for application objects (top) to interact with it. The Pinocchio runtime (right) consists of meta-level objects sending messages, just like application objects. Application objects can fully interact with meta-level objects. Meta-level objects can be replaced by at run time to realize extensions.

The essential ingredients to run-time extensibility in Pinocchio are: (i) a *self-supporting* runtime; (ii) a *message sending* invocation conventions; and (iii) *unification* of meta- and base-level execution.

A self-supporting runtime. The Pinocchio runtime is implemented in a metacircular fashion, so it relies on itself to provide the meta-level facilities needed for its own execution. The Pinocchio runtime is compiled to machine code, resulting in a runtime library rather than a conventional VM.

Message sending invocation conventions. The Pinocchio runtime only hardwires the most essential meta-level facilities needed to support dynamic languages, particularly message sending. Pinocchio provides a meta-level invoke function to lookup a method when an object received a message (see subsection 4.2.2). Method lookup makes use of a monomorphic inline cache. This cache can be pre-filled at compile time, thus avoiding infinite meta-regression when the runtime evaluates itself.

Unification of meta- and base-level execution. The Pinocchio runtime is fully specified in Smalltalk. The Pinocchio compiler compiles the runtime down to machine code, yielding a fully object-oriented runtime library. In essence, the compiler builds the MOP from the Smalltalk sources. As a consequence, the language meta-level is unified with use code, allowing one to move freely between the base- and the meta-level. Furthermore, the meta-level objects, being accessible, can be replaced at run time by compatible application code, thus enabling run-time adaptations.

4.2 See Pinocchio Run

In this section we explain in greater detail the design and implementation of the Pinocchio runtime.

Pinocchio sets up the runtime of Smalltalk applications in the same style as runtimes of C- and C++-based applications. Smalltalk applications are natively compiled, and supported by a meta-circularly implemented runtime library. However, unlike VM-based environments it is designed as a language-agnostic environment. Every object in the runtime can choose its own language semantics. Objects interact with each other without the need to wrap foreign objects. Instead of relying on a bytecode interpreter, the runtime is held together by the following conventions:

Object Headers. Every object is essentially data[2] preceded by a header that contains a pointer to an object describing its *behavior*.

Message sending. Objects can send messages to each other. This is realized by establishing *invocation conventions*, and providing an object-oriented *meta-level* runtime library.

By only specifying an interface for message sending, Pinocchio leaves the door open to interoperability with any other object-oriented language that implements the interface. Since the runtime library is implemented in Smalltalk, a rich meta-object protocol is automatically available to applications. This in turn allows developers to easily implement language extensions, debugging and profiling facilities. It also makes it easier to implement a runtime library for another language in Smalltalk, as an extension of the existing runtime library.

We will now elaborate the following points:

- Invocation conventions (subsection 4.2.1) define how messages are sent between objects.

- Lookup and apply procedures (subsection 4.2.2) provide the semantics of method lookup and execution.

- Infinite meta-regression (subsection 4.2.3) is avoided by pre-filling inline caches.

- Native compilation (subsection 4.2.5) adopts conventional compiler architecture and techniques.

- Bootstrapping Pinocchio (subsection 4.2.6) relies on an existing Smalltalk implementation to cross-compile the runtime.

- Performance (subsection 4.2.7) is assessed with some simple benchmarks.

---

[2]The current implementation of Pinocchio still relies on the Boehm-Demers-Weiser conservative garbage collector. However, care has been taken to lay out all Smalltalk objects so that they could be managed by a precise garbage collector.

4.2.1 Invocation Conventions

Message sending in Pinocchio is mapped to native calls. The calls follow invocation conventions that define how to set up the receiver, message and arguments, and how to save and restore the environment for method invocation. The conventions are an extension to the calling conventions defined by the operating system ABI (application binary interface). They provide the protocol for arbitrary callers and callees to send and receive messages. Pinocchio method invocations rely on monomorphic inline caches, explained in subsection 2.1.3.

In essence, the following Smalltalk message send:

```
bank accept: money
```

is translated to the native X86-64 equivalent of the following pseudo-code:

```
invoke(#accept:, bank, money);
```

As explained in subsection 2.1.3, the `invoke` function is a meta-level function that supports the initial method lookup and activation. To fill the inline cache for the type Bank, it is dynamically replaced with:

```
Bank>>accept:(Bank, bank, money);
```

4.2.2 Lookup and Apply

The `invoke` function is the entry point to the meta-level lookup implementation. It first reads out the behavior object associated with the receiver from its object header. Then it looks up the selector in the behavior, and applies the resulting method to the receiver[3].

```
invoke: selector
    <invoke>
    |method behavior|
    behavior ← self behavior.
    method ← behavior lookup: selector for: self.
    ↑ method perform: selector on: self.
```

Listing 4.1: The `invoke` method in pseudo-Smalltalk.

Listing 4.1 implements the default `invoke` function. The `<invoke>` annotation informs the compiler that this is a special meta-level method that is activated to support a base-level method invocation. It instructs the compiler to generate code that preserves all volatile argument registers before executing the method body[4]. Secondly it tells the compiler that this method needs access to the selector rather than other arguments. Since Smalltalk

---
[3] Filling in the inline cache is part of the application mechanism.
[4] This is analogous to a *syscall* in UNIX, where another execution level is entered and the calling environment has to be preserved.

only relies on the receiver and the selector to dispatch a message, the default invoke-compiler only makes those values available to the invoke metamethod. Finally, it enables the compiler's direct support for the perform:on: message, inlining the implementation for standard Smalltalk methods and generating the fallback message send code.

The invoke method is special since it is hardwired in all unlinked Smalltalk send sites and inline cache miss handlers. Its implementation cannot be dynamically configured by receivers, since the sender rather than the receiver chooses its implementation. Thus this method imposes the following minimal requirements on all objects used as receivers:

- All receivers have an object header referring to its behavior, and

- behavior objects are (indirectly) described by SmalltalkBehavior[5].

The actual lookup is performed by the behavior object of the receiver. This is by default an instance of SmalltalkBehavior which implements a single inheritance lookup of the method through the class hierarchy chain. The implementation of this method is shown in listing 4.2. As we will show later this object can be exchanged by a user to redefine the semantics of message lookup.

```
lookup: selector for: object
    |behavior dictionary|
    behavior ← self.
    [ behavior == nil ] whileFalse: [
        dictionary ← behavior methodDictionary.
        (dictionary at: selector)
            ifNotNil: [ :method | ↑ method ].
        behavior ← behavior super ].
    ↑ self doesNotUnderstand
```

Listing 4.2: A meta-level lookup method that browses a class hierarchy and searches for a matching method.

It is important to stress that this code executes exactly as expected as Smalltalk code. Independently of the exact runtime type of each of the variables, the code will succeed as long as the required messages are understood. For example in Pinocchio a class can have any kind of method dictionary implementation. As long as the *at:* message is understood, and an object is returned that adheres to the interface designated for methods, the message send will succeed. The Pinocchio meta-level has no hard-coded assumptions whatsoever about the method dictionary.

---

[5]This could later be generalized by only requiring a more general LanguageBehavior metabehavior.

4.2.3 Avoiding Meta-regression by Prefilling Inline Caches

The meta-level of Pinocchio is written in pure Smalltalk, and thus can support its own execution — it is its own meta-level. This however conceptually results in infinite *meta-regression* caused by *self-referencing code* [39]. The meta-level `invoke` shown in listing 4.1, for example, implements method lookup using message sends. Those messages require method lookups as well. This implies that all messages sent during an `invoke` will also call `invoke`, causing meta-regression.

To solve this problem, we differentiate between formal and actual binding time. This notion was introduced by Malenfant [98]:

> "A **formal binding** time is the latest moment at which a binding can occur in general, while an **actual binding time** is the actual moment at which the binding occurs for a particular element of a particular program." [98]

The semantics of Pinocchio are realised only with late-bound message sends. While in some cases we shift the actual binding of a message send to compile time, the formal binding stays at run time. For example, just like in Self [30], our compiler inlines `ifTrue:ifFalse:` for the expected values `true` and `false` by performing local jumps. However, rather than implementing it as an if/else branch, there is a third case where the receiver is neither `true` nor `false`. In that case a message is sent to the actual receiver. This provides the illusion that the message is actually implemented as a message send, thus maintaining the formal binding time while improving performance through inlining.

Meta-regression resulting from sending messages is solved in a similar way. We shift the actual binding time for meta-level message sends from run time to compile-time by pre-filling a minimal number of inline caches, effectively turning late-bound message sends into early-bound calls with late-bound fallback. It ensures that the default execution path for message lookup and invocation is directly accessible without triggering meta-regression. By relying on inline caches to hardwire the meta-level, Pinocchio preserves the semantics of all message-sends at the meta-level by design, essentially unifying the meta-level with the base-level.

This is implemented as follows. First we ensure that every message sent across the entire default method lookup path has a variable (as opposed to a more complex expression) as receiver. This includes the `behavior` variable in the `invoke:` method, but also other variables such as the `dictionary` variable in the `lookup:` method, and the `bucket` variable in the `at:` method. We then manually annotate all those variables with the following type hints:

`<typeHint: #dictionary as: #MethodDictionary>`

Rather than calling `invoke`, the compiler statically links the send sites to the methods that are looked up in the hinted classes at compile-time. Finally, pre-filled inline caches are immutable, which is necessary to ensure that the base case is not unlinked by a non-default meta-object. This is achieved by performing the type check at the send site and skipping the preamble of the pre-filled method. This implementation implies that inlined methods must be regular methods with a regular preamble.

In the previous example, messages sent to the variable `dictionary` will assume it is of type `MethodDictionary`. Instead of calling `invoke` and passing the symbol `#at:`, the send site will first check if the receiver is of type `MethodDictionary`. If so, it calls the `MethodDictionary`'s `at:` method, bypassing the preamble of the method. If it fails however, a regular caching send site is activated. The type check ensures that the formal binding time stays at run time.

The type hints are visible inside the meta code and therefore explicitly document the default control flow. They are not external assumptions but are specified from within the runtime. The Pinocchio MOP is *anchored* by annotated default meta-objects. The statically defined anchors in the Pinocchio runtime are merely base cases, however, hardwired to avoid recursion. They only provide an early-bound native execution flow without influencing the formal binding time. They can be overloaded with custom code at any level of meta-regression, and thus preserve the semantics of message sends.

4.2.4 Separation of Class and Behavior

The use of type hints for meta-level code impacts the design of the meta-level. Pinocchio does not directly use classes to store the behavior of objects. The problem with Smalltalk classes is that each class is an instance of its own meta-class. This renders it impossible to pre-fill the inline cache for the message sent during `invoke` to lookup the method. If `lookup:for:` would be sent to the class, it would result mostly in cache misses, since different classes have different meta-classes.

Instead, Pinocchio installs the behavior of objects in explicit behavior metaobjects. As shown in Figure 4.2, the header of an object points to the behavior containing the method dictionary, rather than to the class. These behavior metaobjects are generally instances of the class `SmalltalkBehavior`. Hence we pre-fill the behavior-related inline caches in the meta-level `invoke` with `SmalltalkBehavior` methods. To model the normal Smalltalk class hierarchy, and to support class-side methods, every `SmalltalkBehavior` instance links to the related first-class class metaobject.

4.2.5 Native Compilation

The Pinocchio compiler is fully written in Smalltalk and currently supports System V AMD64 (Linux and OSX on X86-64). By targeting the runtime directly towards the CPU as its execution environment we minimize assumptions about the supported language. The compiler has a fairly traditional

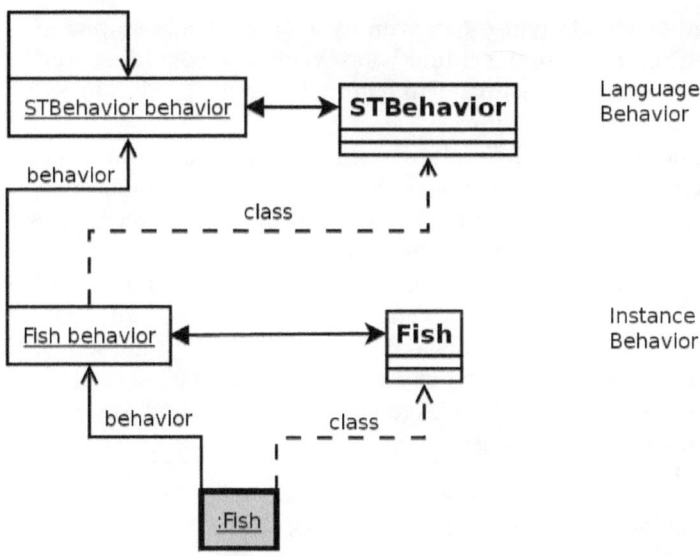

Figure 4.2: The class side of an object is modelled by two entities: the behavior instance which contains the methods and implements the lookup semantics and the class which is the first-class representation of the class. It contains the class-side methods and can have a custom meta-class.

architecture: methods are parsed by a *parsing expression grammar* [61] into an abstract syntax tree (AST). We apply semantic analysis on variables while transforming the AST into three address code (TAC). After applying a *linear scan register allocator* [118] and some easy peephole optimizations, the assembler generates the X86-64 binary instructions. The resulting method object has a memory layout similar to the format used by Squeak and Pharo: the object header is followed by a list of literals, and then native code stored as an array of bytes.

Local variables are mapped onto registers, spilled onto the stack or captured in remote arrays (see subsection 2.4.3. Instance variable accesses are implemented by reading out the receiver as an array. Literals used in the method are read using *position-independent code*[6] (PIC), accessed relative to the instruction pointer. Because method invocations are mapped onto native calls, the native stack is used as our Smalltalk call stack. Since the size of method frames can be statically determined for Smalltalk methods, we use the *base pointer* register as general-purpose register and only rely on the *stack pointer* for keeping track of the call stack[7].

---

[6]By relying on position-independent instructions for literal loading we minimize the number of instructions that need to be updated when a compacting garbage collector moves the code in memory. Call targets will still need to be updated however since objects move independently of each other.

[7]This is equivalent to the `-fomit-frame-pointer` optimization used by GCC.

Our implementation also has primitives. They can be implemented either by letting the compiler inline hand-written three address code or by linking to an external function. This external function just has to be linkable and follow our call conventions.

Pinocchio message sends follow standard calling conventions (see subsection 4.2.1), and rely on monomorphic inline caches (see subsection 2.1.3). The advantage of following the standard ABI calling conventions is that it is easy to link to library code written in C or assembler. As long as code follows the conventions and takes pointers to objects as arguments, it behaves like a valid method. Another advantage is that it allows calls to Pinocchio code to be interleaved with calls to C code. By following the same conventions we ensure that the context of the callee is always preserved.

We compile method preambles to one of three different formats for code size and performance reasons:

- Methods installed on `SmallInteger` bail out if the receiver is not a tagged integer (10 bytes, 2 instructions),

- those installed on classes unrelated to the hierarchy of `SmallInteger` bail out if the receiver is a tagged pointer, or if the class passed via the `%rax` register does not match the class of the receiver (20 bytes, 4 instructions), and

- the methods installed in a superclass of `SmallInteger` have the full preamble that combines both previous approaches (30 bytes, 7 instructions).

4.2.6 Bootstrapping Pinocchio

Currently, the Pinocchio runtime is cross-compiled runtime from within the Pharo Smalltalk environment, although the goal is to self-host the compiler, making it available at run time as well.

Pinocchio is bootstrapped by constructing a minimal Smalltalk image. This is implemented by recursively gathering all relevant classes and compiling their methods within Pharo. The compiler caches symbols it finds during compilation in a symbol table. The image is then serialized into separate relocatable object files. Our serializer currently supports the ELF and Mach-O formats. All classes and their related objects are written out to a single relocatable object file per class. These object files include the class, its metaclass, the method dictionaries, and the compiled methods with their literals. Additionally, one object file is created for the symbol table, and another one for the native objects, like `nil` and `true`.

All objects that are referred to across the object file boundary are exported as relocatable objects. They are identified using a globally unique identifier in their object file's relocation table. Pointers to the objects are written out as entries into the relocation table, referring to the unique identifier. This is shown in Figure 4.3. The final image is then constructed by linking the object files using the standard GNU linker (ld). The resulting binary is similar to a normal Smalltalk image containing all objects required by the system, with the difference that it is fully self-contained by including the whole runtime as well.

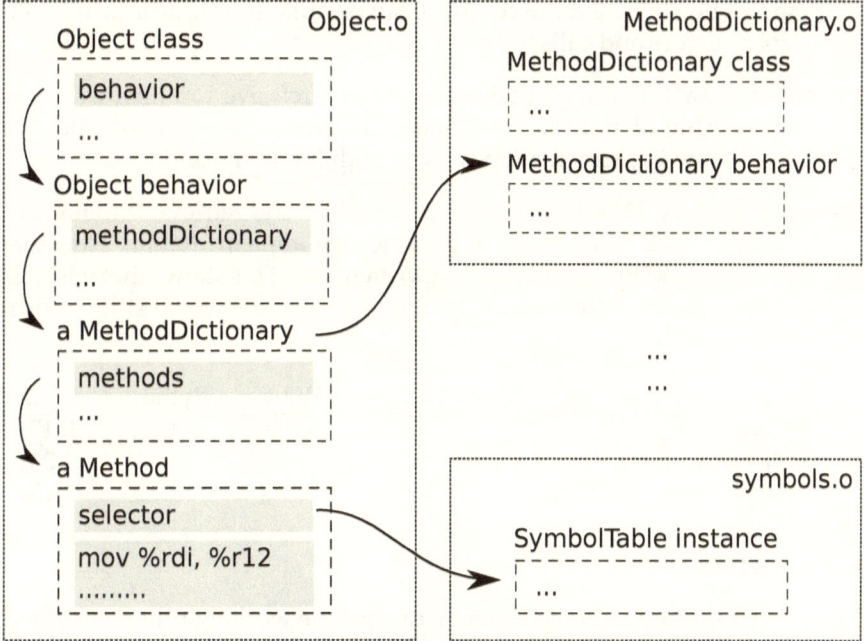

Figure 4.3: Pinocchio binaries layout. Arrows represent linked objects. Every object has a header that links to its class (not all links shown).

To start up the resulting system there is no additional bootstrapping required. Since we follow the ABI standards, the operating system sets up the runtime by loading the binary into memory and calling the first function.

4.2.7 Performance

To show that a metacircular runtime can compete with the performance of current dynamic language implementations, we run three simple benchmarks. They do not thoroughly benchmark the runtime, but are merely meant as an indicator of the performance of specific but commonly used functions. We especially focus on the performance of message sending, given that it is the topic of this chapter, and avoid performance related to object allocation, given that we currently still rely on an external memory manager.

We compare Pinocchio with Ruby version 1.9.2-p290, Python version 2.6.7 and the Croquet Closure Cog VM version 4.0-2489. Cog is a modern

JIT VM for Smalltalk[8]. The results are the average of 10 consecutive runs. The benchmarks are:

Fibonacci(35) The time it takes to recursively calculate the 35th Fibonacci number. Since all messages sent can be inline cached this mainly shows how efficient the compiler can compile simple arithmetic, control structure and calls.

PDictionary(1M) The time it takes to store and retrieve 1 million entries in a Pinocchio dictionary. The Pinocchio dictionary was used since the exact same implementation runs on both Pinocchio and Cog.

NativeDictionary(1M) The time it takes to store and retrieve 1 million entries in a dictionary native to the language implementation. Note that the Ruby and Python hashes are written in C! This shows that it is possible to have metacircular core language features which still perform well enough.

	Pinocchio	Ruby	Python	Cog
Fibonacci(35)	0.22s	1.58s	4.23s	0.17s
PDictionary(1M)	0.96s			1.26s
NativeDictionary(1M)	0.96s	0.86s	0.22s	1.15s

4.2.8 Metrics

The current version of Pinocchio took two people working full time around 4 months to implement. It consists of 17K lines of Smalltalk code, 600 lines of C code (of which 20% is support code for inspecting objects and debugging the runtime in GDB, another 10% are memory management functions, and the rest are Smalltalk primitives) and 50 lines of assembler code that supports the `invoke` method.

The Smalltalk code consists of the following parts:

	KLOC
Parser	3.5
Three Address Code generation	4.5
Assembler	1.5
Class building and linking	0.5
ELF/Mach-O back-end	3.5
Smalltalk runtime objects	3
Examples	0.5

4.3 Evaluation and applications

To support our claims regarding Pinocchio's extensibility, its reconfigurability and its potential for reuse, in this section we provide several examples.

---

[8]see http://www.mirandabanda.org/cog/

4.3.1 Reconfiguring the meta-level

The following examples highlight Pinocchio's flexible metacircular meta-level that safeguards encapsulation by only relying on message sends. They show how a user can intercept method invocations by injecting his own meta-objects into the meta-level.

Tracing method activations. Suppose a developer wants to trace accept: messages sent to Bank instances. This can be implemented by customizing the meta-objects: The accept: method in the Bank's method dictionary is wrapped in a proxy object that logs the messages before activating the method:

```
perform: selector on: receiver with: args
    logger logMessage: selector to: receiver with: args.
    ↑ originalMethod perform: selector on: receiver with: args
```

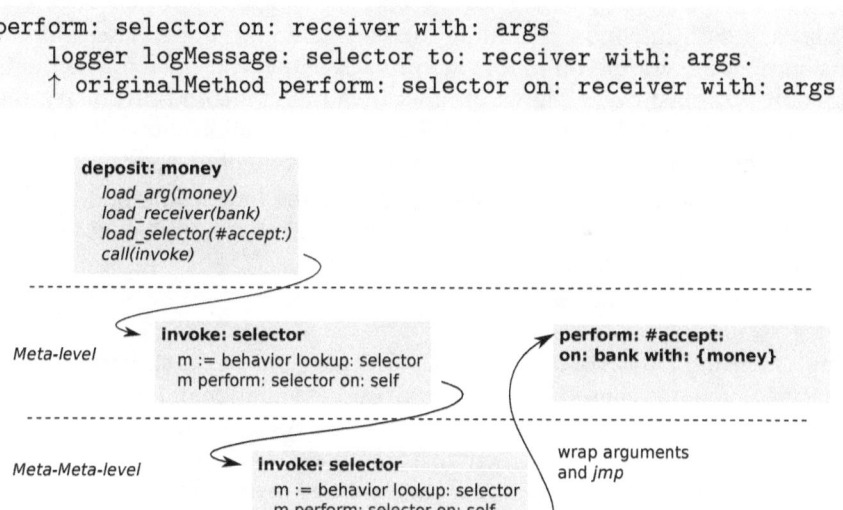

Figure 4.4: The evaluation of invoke in the case of a custom method object. Invoke will send the message *perform:on:with* to the method instead of directly jumping to the method. Note that there are conceptually two meta-levels, but the meta-meta-level is in fact the same as the meta-level since it is self supporting.

This is supported by the invoke implementation shown in Listing 4.1. After invoke looks up the method, it applies this method to the receiver by sending it perform:on:. As explained in subsection 4.2.2, the <invoke> annotation causes the compiler to specialize this message into two distinct cases. Native methods are executed directly by jumping to the native code. All other objects receive the message perform: selector on: receiver with: arguments from the invoke method. In this message the original arguments are wrapped into an array since Smalltalk methods do not support a variable number of arguments. This is handled by custom glue code in the `invoke` function. Figure 4.4 shows the execution path of a Bank instance receiving the `accept:` message and activating the wrapped method.

Tracing single objects.   To trace all messages sent to a single object we can customize its meta-level behavior. This is implemented by replacing its behavior with an instance of a subclass of `SmalltalkBehavior` that specializes the `lookup:for:` method. This method automatically wraps all retrieved methods into logging proxy objects:

```
lookup: selector for: object
    method ← super lookup: selector for: object.
    ↑ MessageLogProxy wrap: method
```

This causes all methods, including methods found in superclasses of the instance, to be wrapped into logging proxies. However, since the methods are only wrapped during lookup rather than in the method dictionary, the changes only affect the traced object. This implementation shows that meta-level functionality can be reused just like regular Smalltalk code.

Other possible applications of customizing the lookup method include debugging, profiling, object-sensitive access control, message queuing and remote method invocation.

Implementing DoesNotUnderstand.   The `perform:on:with:` protocol for applying methods is used inside the core implementation of Pinocchio itself — namely to implement `doesNotUnderstand:`. As in regular Smalltalk implementations, if a message is sent to a Smalltalk object that does not implement it, `doesNotUnderstand: originalMessage` is sent instead. The implementation of this protocol is only a few lines in Pinocchio: If no method can be found, the lookup method of `SmalltalkBehavior` returns an instance of `DoesNotUnderstand` instead. This `DoesNotUnderstand` instance implements the `perform:on:with:` method as follows:

```
perform: aSelector on: receiver with: someArguments
    message ← Message new.
    message arguments: someArguments.
    message selector: aSelector.
    ↑ receiver doesNotUnderstand: message
```

This example shows how a language feature, otherwise hardwired in the VM, can be implemented inside the runtime environment. No support from an external lower level is required, and any developer can add such a protocol to his meta-level.

4.3.2 Changing lookup semantics

By adding a new behavior implementation we can completely alter the way messages are looked up. We show this by implementing prototype-based method lookup. This `PrototypeBehavior` can be installed on an existing object, transforming it into a prototype. Prototypes carry their own method dictionary, called `slots`, can clone themselves and delegate messages to the object they were cloned from.

`PrototypeBehavior` implements the lookup as follows:

```
lookup: selector for: object
    | currentObj |
    (primitiveMethods at: selector)
        "if the method is primitive, use it"
        ifNotNil: [ :method | ↑ method ].

    currentObj ← object.
    [currentObj == nil] whileFalse: [
        (currentObj slot: selector)
            "if I have the method, use it"
            ifNotNil: [ :method | ↑ method ].
        "else look in my delegate chain"
        currentObj ← currentObj delegate ].

    ↑ DoesNotUnderstand new "whoops -- nothing found"
```

The behavior holds a set of primitive methods that are used for interacting with prototypes, namely `slot:`, `delegate` and `clone`. While we could have used type hinting to bootstrap those messages, as described in the previous section, here we use the classical approach: We rely on the bootstrapped Smalltalk system to store the primitive methods.

Objects are converted to prototypes by replacing their behavior:

`prototypeObject behavior: aPrototypeBehavior`

After executing the previous code, `prototypeObject` will have prototype-like semantics and therefore behave like an object from a different language. It will not even understand the message `class`. Other instances in the runtime are unaffected by this modification. The `PrototypeBehavior` that implements the prototype semantics, for example, behaves like a regular Smalltalk object. Thanks to the invocation conventions, however, both types of objects can freely interact with each other by sending messages, even if those messages are handled by different meta-levels.

4.4 Discussion

There are widely perceived advantages to the traditional bytecode-based virtual machine approach that we did not yet address directly, such as portability, debugging, instrumentation, and security. In this section we discuss how we envision to support these features within the Pinocchio runtime. Additionally we explain how all the advantages of VMs over native compilation fade in the presence of JIT compilation.

Portability across platforms is one of the most important advantages of a traditional VM. After porting the VM to multiple platforms, the "binary" bytecode files supported by the VM are automatically supported by these platforms.

All real-world high-performance VMs JIT compile the code they receive to native code. D'Hondt argued [42] that bytecodes are not an ideal format for these purposes. We see *slim binaries* [64] as a more interesting source of code input. Slim binaries are a highly compact, architecture-independent intermediate code representation optimized to be the input for a JIT compiler which then targets a specific architecture. By not only being portable, but also more high-level, slim binaries offer a better portable code source format than bytecode for later optimization. Since slim binaries are more high-level, other tasks such as code validation may become easier as well. Slim binaries were originally proposed as alternative to *fat binaries* containing native code for all possible target architectures.

While a VM enhances portability of applications, the VM itself can be quite hard to port to a new architecture. Additionally, the JIT compiler will have to be customized towards the new platform. As shown by the Klein project, in contrast to a VM written in a low-level language, a clean metacircular and object-oriented VM design eases porting to a different hardware platform [143].

Debugging programs that run on VMs or interpreters is often considered to be easier than debugging native applications. Interpreters can provide reflective hooks to the runtime behavior of an application required to understand how the application executes.

In JIT compiled runtimes, however, the VM needs to bridge the gap back from native compiled code to the original bytecode. Since the bytecode is most likely not the source code format used by the developer, this again needs to be linked back to the language of origin. Especially when a runtime hosts many languages, this requires external meta-data about the application that is running.

Native applications on the Linux platform can be compiled to contain extra meta-data about the native code, in a language-agnostic, standardized debugging data format called DWARF [50]. This format is for example supported by the GNU Project Debugger, GDB. Kell and Irwin [83] demonstrated with their DwarfPython [83] how this format can be successfully used to debug dynamic applications implemented in Python. Additionally, by relying on a standard debugging format, multiple languages can be debugged in an interleaved fashion. This is exemplified by debugging C and Python within the same debugger.

Pinocchio currently does not dynamically generate DWARF meta-data, nor meta-data for understanding native functions, but our exporter does generate method names in the exported object files. This currently allows us to debug Smalltalk applications with an understanding of the call-stack through GDB.

We do not of course see GDB as the final goal for debugging dynamic applications. However, since meta-data is available we can build custom debuggers around the standardized meta-data. This will not only benefit the languages we support, but others as well, as long as they follow the standard.

Instrumentation of language-level operations is potentially made easier by having units in the VM that can be edited to perform extra work. This has for example been used to build a practical back-in-time debugger that works by tracking object flow [94].

This approach however is only practical as long as the VM is used as a vanilla interpreter. Once JIT compilation comes into play, the JIT compiler needs to be aware of the extra payload introduced by the semantic changes of the user.

Sub-method reflection [37] is an approach that provides direct access to the semantics of language and sub-method level operations. It provides a reflective interface to methods at the AST level, even though they actually execute at a lower level. The availability of a sub-method reflective interface and code weaving can be used as an alternative to having direct access to the VM code.

A secondary advantage to instrumentation in the VM is that, since the instrumentation code is written at another level, the instrumentation code itself is immune to its own modifications. However, even in the case of the back-in-time debugger, much of the debugging code itself was written within the language that ran on top of the VM. This forced the developers to add a hook to turn the extensions to the VM off whenever the debugger was running, to avoid tracking the state of the debugger.

By explicitly representing the meta-level in the form of *meta-context* objects [38], extensions installed through sub-method reflection can be prevented from triggering themselves.

Security is a valuable feature attributed to VMs. By viewing the VM as a *trust root* we can use it to enforce and govern security policies, *e.g.*, through bytecode verification [91].

We argue that any piece of software can potentially be used as a trust root. For example the system's class loading library can verify the code in slim binary or even native code. A compiler that can generate malicious code should only be available to the runtime during development. And as shown by Miller and Gough [103], object-capabilities [103] support such an alternative security model at runtime. Newspeak showed that a secure language can be built using this approach. The architecture relies on mirrors [23] to limit the accessible scope of runtime capabilities to an end-user only by enforcing encapsulation.

Additionally, giving a developer access to the meta-level of a language enables him to introduce new kind of policies and restrictions tailored to his needs. For example Fischer *et al.* [58] present a model object level access control [58]. The introduced policies work by restricting object access more tightly. In an open system a developer could extend the meta-behavior himself to accompany such run-time checks without depending on VM support.

4.5 Related Work

As described in detail in Section 3.2, the Klein project implement a meta-circular VM [143] by hardwiring the layout of objects, declare that every object is described by a map, and break meta-recursion by hardwiring a single *map of maps*. Method lookup is however directly implemented in a very low-level subset of Self. Unlike Pinocchio message lookup, the resulting lookup does not support polymorphic behavior, but is hardwired towards standard maps.

Piumarta and Warth [117] propose a flexible object model [115, 117] based on *v-tables* that describe the behavior an object. Similar to the work by Malenfant [97], rather than hardwiring the lookup of methods for all v-tables, it only relies on native lookup support for v-tables described by the so-called *v-table of v-tables*. Methods returned from a v-table are native functions. Neither the inner shape of objects nor the behavior contained in methods is defined by the system. In Pinocchio we adopted the message sending interface based on v-tables (the object header) as the basis for language independence. We do not however rely on a hardwired meta-meta-level but rather teach the meta-level to support itself. This means that the meta-level itself is defined in terms of Smalltalk polymorphic message sends and provides a rich meta-object protocol.

DwarfPython [83] unifies the object model of Python with native C-structs by interpreting the DWARF meta-data [83]. The AST-interpreter is extended to interpret DWARF meta-information describing how to access objects. This allows DwarfPython code to automatically interact with foreign functions since it can interpret the resulting data. By generating native entry points and DWARF meta-data for Python functions, the code interface between Python and C is unified. This provides a two-way interface between native and Python code, and allows developers to rely on GDB for debugging. Pinocchio currently cannot interact with data that does not have an object header. Additionally it lacks proper meta-descriptions to implement cross-language debugging. Our focus is however on providing an extensible framework for implementing self-supporting languages which is lacking in DwarfPython.

4.6 Summary

In this chapter we showed how the meta-level of a language can be unified with normal user-level code. Instead of having an artificial separation between meta- and base-level objects can freely pass between the two. All source code is compiled to machine code. Pinocchio maintains the semantics of message sends to the greatest possible degree, thus avoiding the need for an explicit change in meta-level. By replacing an object of the Pinocchio MOP new behavior or new reflective capabilities can be added. The shift in meta-levels is implicit, conforming to the conventional meta-model of class-based inheritance and message sending between objects.

We were able to show how this approach enables a user to extend the runtime to his needs through some typical examples. Furthermore we could also demonstrate that the performance impact of having metacircular implementations for core language features is not too big. We even gain performance by compiling directly to binary.

This first building block of programming languages separates the language semantics at the object boundary. Each side of the interaction can freely choose its own language semantics. The semantics of message lookup are supported by providing a first-class message lookup library that can be customized as needed. In the next chapter, we will support per-object language customization by augmenting this model with a first-class library for specifying the layouts of objects.

Chapter 4. First-Class Message Lookup

5
First-Class Object Layouts

The previous chapter provided a framework for customizing the semantics of message passing on a per-object basis. In this chapter we provide individuality in the dimension of state. We decouple the structure declaration of objects from the low-level view. We introduce *object layouts*, *layout scopes* and *slots* as first-class building blocks that bridge the gap between the primitive object representation of the garbage collector and its semantics within the programming language. It is constrained by the requirements of the GC, but is open-ended on the language side, allowing languages to easily support new semantics below the granularity of classes. Languages can expose the model to their users, allowing them to built custom language extensions, in most cases without the need to modify the compiler or class builder.

The contributions of this chapter are:

- introducing flexible object layouts, metaobjects that describe the structure of objects, and the semantics of initializing and accessing data within the objects,

- presenting a classification and examples of customized slots and their associated behavior,

- introducing and discussing an implementation of the flexible object layouts in Pharo Smalltalk [15]. By implementing flexible object layouts on top of Pharo, we show that they can be supported by existing languages without the need to modify the underlying VM.

Outline Section 5.1 introduces our approach of *flexible object layouts* in which object fields are represented by first-class *slots*. In Section 5.2 we present a series of examples of different kinds of slots with their associated behavior. Section 5.3 illustrates how first-class layout scopes are used to control the visibility of slots. Section 5.4 shows how *stateful traits* are implemented using first-class layouts. In Section 5.6 we shed light on how to build and migrate classes based on layouts. In Section 5.7 we discuss related work.

5.1 Flexible Object Layouts in a Nutshell

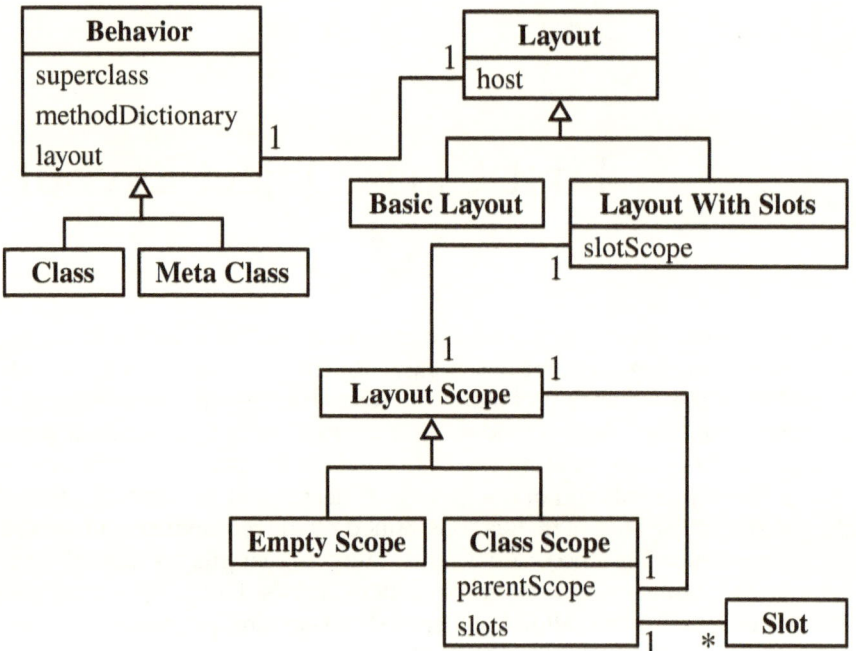

Figure 5.1: Flexible Object Layouts Overview

Tools like compilers and class builders are needed to build up the definition of objects. They are necessarily linked to the runtime that they target. If they are however too tightly coupled to the assumptions made in the VM they become less extensible. By introducing first-class object layouts as building blocks for the programming language, we decouple language tools and the runtime. This layer consists of three main concepts, directly related to the low-level view of how classes are constructed: layouts, layout scopes and slots.

Layouts are the direct reification of the object formats supported by the GC. Just like languages generally store the used object format in the class of an object, we store a single layout instance in each class. A class knows its layout, and the layout knows the class to which it belongs. As shown in Figure 5.1, layouts are installed in the layout instance variable of Class Behavior, the superclass of both Class and Metaclass. The layout itself links back to the Class Behavior through the host instance variable.

The number of available layout types depends on the VM. Our prototype implementation is implemented in the Pharo Smalltalk dialect and provides a fairly typical set of object types: words, bytes, pointers, variable sized, weak pointers, compiled methods, and small integers [65]. Pharo additionally relies on compact classes to save memory for the instances of widely used classes by not keeping a pointer from an instance to a class. All this information encoded in the object header, which is normally only available to the VM, is now directly available in the first-class layout.

Layout scopes group related instance variables. Apart from a few special cases, most classes declare a collection of instance variables. Such classes are related to a *layout with slots*. A class inherits instance variables from its superclass and potentially adds several itself. In our abstraction layer, this is directly modeled using layout scopes. The different layout scopes are nested in a hierarchy parallel to that of the class structure. As Figure 5.1 shows, layout scopes are contained by layouts with slots.

Slots are a first-class representation of instance variables and their corresponding fields[1]. They are referred to by a program's source code when their name is mentioned in an instance variable access. As such they can modify read and write access to fields. In our current implementation the access semantics defined by the slots are directly inlined by the compiler. As Figure 5.1 shows, slots are contained by layout scopes.

Figure 5.2 illustrates our model using the layout of Dictionary. This particular class builds instances with a total of two fields, related to the instance variables #tally and #buckets. Classes that build such instances with a fixed size have a Pointer Layout. Since this layout is a subclass of Layout With Slots, it is related to a *class scope*. Since Dictionary is a subclass of Hashed Collection, the class scope of Dictionary has as parentScope the class scope of Hashed Collection. Because Hashed Collection has two direct instance variables #tally and #buckets, they are linked as slots from the related class scope. Since Object has no slots, its class scope is empty. A list of scopes generally ends in the *empty scope,* just like lists end in nil.

---

[1] For clarity we refer to the memory location in an object as the *field*. The token in source code that refers to the field we call *instance variable*.

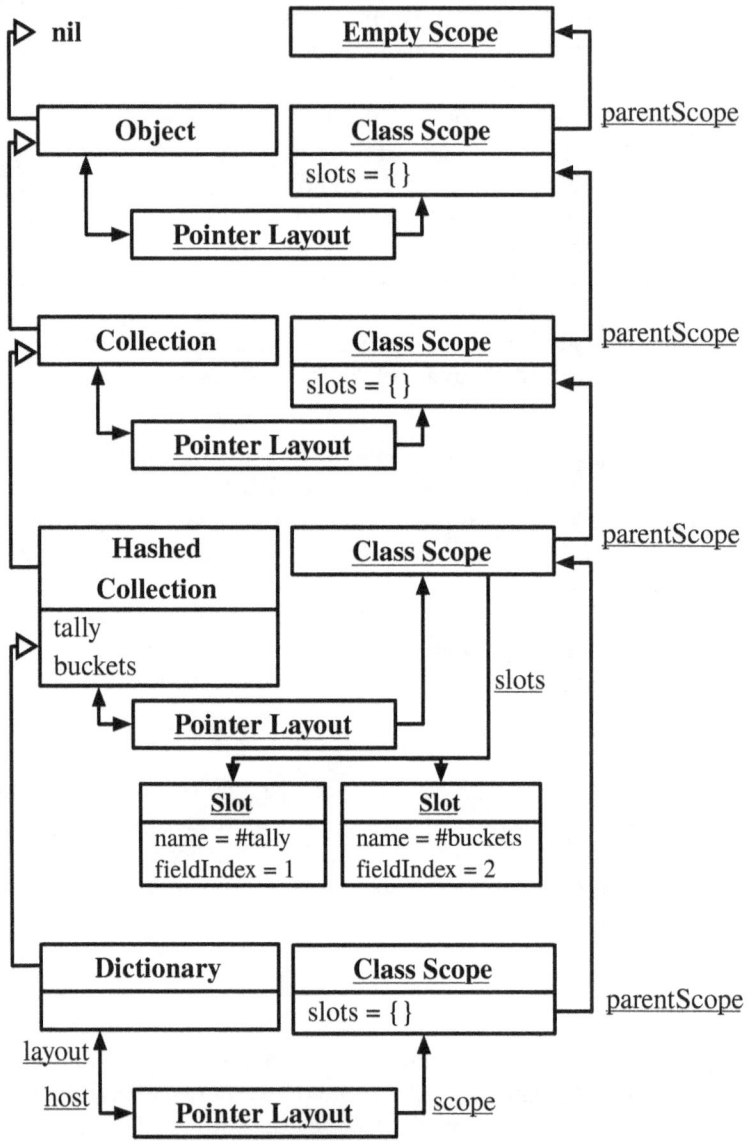

Figure 5.2: Scopes related to `Dictionary`

5.2 First-Class Slots

While normally it is the compiler that is solely responsible for mapping instance variables to fields, slots provide an abstraction that can assume this responsibility. This allows the slots to influence the semantics of accessing instance variables. We distinguish between four types of actions: initialization, reading, writing and migration. Slots can specialize the semantics of any of these four actions by overriding the related method in the slot class definition.

We classify slots as follows:

- *Primitive slots* are the direct reification of the link between instance variables and fields.

- *Customized slots* define custom semantics for the four main actions related to slots: initialization, reading, writing and migration.

- *Virtual slots* have no direct representation in the related objects but rather read state from an aliased field or derive their state in another way.

5.2.1 Primitive Slots

Primitive slots are metaobjects that simply bind an instance variable to a field index.

```
Object subclass: #Slot
    layout: PointerLayout
    slots: {
        #index => Slot.
        #name => Slot.
    }.

Slot >> initializeInstance: anInstance
    self write: nil to: anInstance

Slot >> read: anInstance
    ↑ anInstance instVarAt: index.

Slot >> write: aValue to: anInstance
    ↑ anInstance instVarAt: index put: aValue.
```
Listing 5.1: Default Slot Implementation

Instance variables are by default replaced by standard `Slot` instances. Listing 5.1 shows the core implementation of the default Slot with the three actions for slots:

- *Initialize:* The method named `initializeInstance:` is called during object instantiation for all Slots. As in most languages the fields of newly created object are initialized with `nil`.

- *Read:* The `read:` takes the object instance as an argument and uses the low-level `instVarAt:` to directly access the field in the instance.

- *Write:* The `write:to:` method works similar to the `write:` method and delegates the write access to the low-level `instVarAt:put:` operation.

Notice that the slots in the definition of Slot are such standard metaobjects, making the Slot definition a recursive one. As shown in Listing 5.1, to read out a standard slot we need to first access the `index` slot of the slot. But to access the `index` slot, we need to be able to access the `index` slot, and so on.[2] This circularity is however easily broken by letting the VM directly execute it. Slots break the recursion by directly inlining accessor code into the methods that refer to them.

5.2.2 Customized Slots

Whereas accesses to primitive slots immediately translate into accesses to the related field, it is advantageous to be able to customize the semantics of accessing the slot into something more elaborate. There are four main types of actions related to slots: initialization, read, write and migration.

In standard object-oriented code initialization of slots is handled directly in constructor methods. This implies that initialization code needs to be duplicated for similar but different instance variables, independent of the instance variables being present on the same class. By providing an initialization mechanism on the slot metaobject this initialization code is shared between all instance variables related to the same type of slot. The initialization procedure can be further customized towards the class and finally the instance.

By customizing the reading and writing of slots, we influence all source code that accesses the related instance variable. A slot is read by using it as an *rvalue*. This triggers the protocol `slot read: anInstance`. Slots are written to by using them as an *lvalue*, triggering the protocol `slot write: aValue to: anInstance`. This allows developers to create reusable components at the level of instance variables, avoiding the need for boilerplate code to access them.

Finally slots are related to class updates. Whenever instance variables of a class are removed or added this directly impacts the class and its subclasses, their methods and all their instances. While full-blown solutions to class updates are outside the scope of this dissertation, it is important to mention that our model supports the construction of solutions for class updates. Slots can determine how instances should be migrated at the field-level.

---

[2]This is similar to methods. They are conceptually instances of the Method class. While this class could have a method telling the runtime how to execute the method, this equally recurses infinitely.

Type-checked Slots

As a first example Listing 5.2 shows how we can easily build type-checked slots.

```
Slot subclass: #TypedSlot
    layout: PointerLayout
    slots: {
        #type => TypedSlot type: Class.
    }.

TypedSlot >> write: aValue to: anInstance
    (aValue isNil or: [aValue isKindOf: type])
        ifFalse: [ InvalidTypeError signal ]
    ↑ super write: aValue to: anInstance.
```

Listing 5.2: Typed Slot Implementation

Although it is possible to provide the same functionality as slots by implementing accessor methods, this does not provide the same level of abstraction. It is not possible to enforce that all code indirectly accesses the state over a getter method. Each instance variable requiring preconditions to be fulfilled can also be used in a direct way, circumventing the tests. By relying on slots however, the programmer has only one single way to access the instance variable[3]. Here the guard can be enforced for all methods.

A second advantage of using typed slots rather than relying on modified setter functions is that the semantics of the slot are reified. In the case of typed-checked slots this already provides metadata to gradually add typing to the partly dynamically-typed application, a technique also known as hardening [149].

By encapsulating type checks in slots we can avoid code that would otherwise duplicated. In an untyped language type checks would either occur at instance variable write or in setter methods. Since we can even create a specific slot class for a specific, for example `PositiveIntegerSlot`, there is no need to explicitely type check instance variables anymore.

First-class Relationships

To support first-class relationships in a language, a possible solution is to extend it with first-class support for relationships [14]. However, this burdens language developers with ensuring that all development tools of the host language properly support the language extension, and makes the language more complex than necessary.

Using slots it is possible to model first-class relationships that integrate seamlessly into the existing language. We model relationships by modeling

---

[3]Smalltalk reflection methods, such as `instVarAt:`, could be used to circumvent this mechanism. By solely providing slot objects as reflective mirrors to access state, we can enforce the correct behavior also for reflective access.

both possible sides of *one-to-one*, *one-to-many* and *many-to-many* relationships by defining a One Slot and a Many Slot. To complete the relationship such slots will then have another one or many slot as their *opposite* slot.

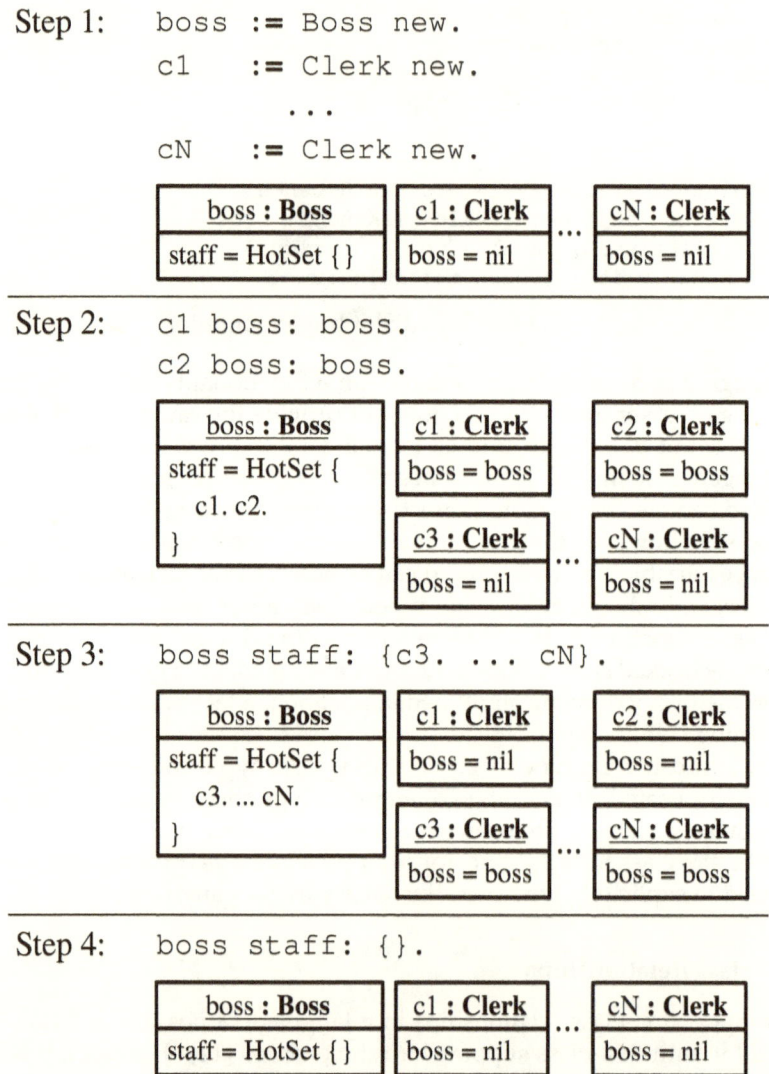

Figure 5.3: Relationships in Action

Listing 5.3 implements two classes Boss and Clerk that are in a one-to-many relationship. A boss has a staff of many clerks, but a clerk just has a single boss. In step 1 of Figure 5.3 we create one instance of the Boss class and N Clerk instances. In step 2 we set the boss of c1 and c2. This makes the boss have two clerks as his staff, and the two clerks have a boss. All the other clerks are unaffected. In step 3 we overwrite the staff by the array of clerks c3 till cN. This breaks the relationship between the boss and c1 and c2 and creates new relationships with the clerks c3 till cN. If in step 4 we set the staff of the boss to the empty array, all relationships are broken again.

```
Object subclass: #Boss
    layout: PointerLayout
    slots: {
        #staff => ManySlot opposite: #boss
                          class: Clerk.
    }

Boss >> staff: aCollection
    staff ← aCollection

Object subclass: #Clerk
    layout: PointerLayout
    slots: {
        #boss => OneSlot opposite: #staff
                         class: Boss.
    }

Clerk >> boss: aBoss
    boss ← aBoss
```

Listing 5.3: Many Relationship Usage

The code in Listing 5.4 shows the full implementation of the related classes. Both ends of a relationship need to be typed, so we reuse the Typed Slot class from Listing 5.2. We extend it by adding a subclass Opposite Slot that knows that both slots that occur in a relationship refer back to each other using the opposite instance variable[4]. Finally the One Slot knows that it will contain a single value, while the Many Slot has many values. To make the picture complete, in the case of a Many Slot we install a *hot collection*. This is a special kind of collection that knows that it has to update the opposite side on every change. This is required since the collection itself is a way to avoid having to directly access the data via the slot.

```
TypedSlot subclass: #OppositeSlot
    layout: PointerLayout
    slots: {
        #opposite => OneSlot opposite: #opposite
                             class: OppositeSlot.
    }

OppositeSlot subclass: #ManySlot
    layout: PointerLayout
```

---

[4]Notice that #opposite is also declared as a One Slot, referring back to itself. This is because a slot #y that has slot #x as its opposite, is by itself the opposite of #x. Slots that are in a relationship at the base-level are also in a relationship on the meta-level.

```
    slots: {
        #oppositeHost => Slot.
    }

ManySlot >> initializeInstance: anInstance
    |set|
    set ← HotSet new
        oppositeSlot: opposite;
        myself: anInstance;
        type: self oppositeHost.
    super internalWrite: set to: anInstance.


ManySlot >> write: aValueCollection to: anObject
    |hotSet|
    hotSet ← self read: anObject.
    hotSet removeAll.

    aValueCollection ensureType: Collection.
    hotSet addAll: aValueCollection.


OppositeSlot subclass: #OneSlot
    layout: PointerLayout
    slots: {}

OneSlot >> write: aValue to: anObject
    (self internalRead: anObject)
        ifNotNilDo: [:oldValue|
            opposite remove: anObject from: oldValue].

    super write: aValue to: anObject.

    aValue ifNotNil: [opposite add: anObject to: aValue].
```

Listing 5.4: Relationship Slot Implementation

There are several advantages to using slots rather than specific language extensions. A library encapsulates the core behavior of relationships but still requires a significant amount of glue code to invoke all necessary hooks. However it is possible to dispense with glue code altogether by implementing the first-class relationships directly as a language extension. But language changes require all the tools to be changed as well. Hence we argue in favor of an implementation which solely requires first-class slots that intercept read and write access, obviating the need to modify tools for slot-related language customizations. As shown in Listing 5.3 it is sufficient to specify the relationship with slots.

5.2.3 Virtual Slots

Virtual slots, unlike the previously presented slots, do not require a field in the related object but redirect access to the data elsewhere.

Alias slots are a trivial kind of virtual slot that simply redirect all accesses to the aliased slots. Listing 5.5 shows the basic implementation details of the alias slot. The basic access operations read: and write:to: are forwarded to aliasedSlot. This is useful for providing a compatibility interface for legacy or external code. Wrongly named variable accesses can be redirected by specifying an alias to an existing slot. Since accesses to the slot are directly compiled as accesses to the aliased slot there is no extra overhead by using an alias slot over a normal one.

```
VirtualSlot subclass: #AliasSlot
    layout: PointerLayout
    slots: {
        #aliasedSlot => TypedSlot type: Slot.
    }.

AliasSlot >> read: anInstance
    ↑ aliasedSlot read: anInstance

AliasSlot >> write: aValue to: anInstance
    ↑ aliasedSlot write: aValue to: anInstance
```

Listing 5.5: Alias Slot Implementation

Derived slots are computed from the values of other slots. They can be used for example to provide a dual representation of values without having to duplicate support code or add explicit transformation code. The code in Listing 5.6 shows a Color object which has three standard slots for the three color compounds red, green and blue. The fourth slot is a virtual slot combining the three compounds into a single integer value. The RGBSlot internally links to the three other color components, denoted by the slots named #r, #g and #b. Internally the RGBSlot uses these slots as sources and transforms the input and output to represent one single integer value.

On assignment the RBG Slot splits the written integer value into the three compounds and forwards them to the corresponding slots. On read access the single integer value is computed from the three other slots. By reading from the rgb instance variable the full combined integer value is read. This has the advantage over a normal method invocation in that it can be directly inlined by the compiler and that it stays private to the class. Whenever this dual number representation is required elsewhere it is sufficient to copy over the RGB Slot and thus the slot helps to reduce code duplication.

```
VirtualSlot subclass: #RGBSlot
    layout: PointerLayout
    slots: {
        #redSlot   => TypedSlot type: Slot.
        #greenSlot => TypedSlot type: Slot.
        #blueSlot  => TypedSlot type: Slot.
    }.

RGBSlot >> read: aColor
    ↑ (((redSlot   read: aColor) & 0xFF) << 16)
    + (((greenSlot read: aColor) & 0xFF) << 8)
    + ((blueSlot   read: aColor) & 0xFF).

RGBSlot >> write: anInt to: aColor
    redSlot   write:((anInt & 0xFF0000) >> 16) to: aColor.
    greenSlot write:((anInt & 0x00FF00) >>  8) to: aColor.
    blueSlot  write: (anInt & 0x0000FF)        to: aColor.


Object subclass: #Color
    layout: PointerLayout
    slots: {
        #r   => PositiveIntSlot limit: 0xFF.
        #g   => PositiveIntSlot limit: 0xFF.
        #b   => PositiveIntSlot limit: 0xFF.
        #rgb => RGBSlot redSlot: #r
                        greenSlot: #g
                        blueSlot: #b.
    }.
```

Listing 5.6: RGB Color Slot Implementation

5.2.4 Implementation and Performance

Slot metaobjects define how instance variables are accessed. This is implemented as follows:

While compiling a method, the compiler fetches the slot metaobject and asks it to generate the access code. The default code in the Slot class inlines the slot object itself and generates the accessing message send to the slot object, with the receiver (and value, in case of assignment) as argument. This default method is useful for quickly prototyping new slots without having to define a code generation strategy, but has the potential overhead of requiring a message send (or function call, once it is inline cached by the underlying runtime), rather than a direct memory access. Once the slot semantics are complex enough, however, this extra cost becomes irrelevant.

Additionally our compiler uses Helvetia [122] as a macro system to easily describe the code required to correctly inline the slot semantics. Primitive slots use this mechanism to generate simple memory access, thus fully eliminating the cost.

5.3 First-Class Layout Scopes

In our system a layout consists of layout scopes, which themselves again can contain slots. Layout scopes provide a level of reusable object semantics that is orthogonal to the standard reuse through subclassing. They are responsible for providing access to instance variables and requiring the fields in the final instance. This allows them to influence the visibility of slots while still requiring enough space for all slots in the final instances. By creating custom layout scopes we can implement more complex use-cases which would otherwise require boilerplate code.

The two core scopes, the empty scope and the class scope are shown in Figure 5.1. As a default for each class a class scope is generated and linked to a parent scope which holds the slots forming the superclass. These layout scopes form a chain which eventually ends in an empty scope, as shown in Figure 5.2. With this approach we have a compatible model to represent slot reuse through subclassing. So far we only assumed that the scopes will contain exactly the slots from the class definition. The following examples however, show situations where new slots are introduced depending on the slots specified in the class definition. We introduce additional slots by adding specialized scopes. Hence the class scopes always contain exactly the scopes provided with the class definition.

In addition to the empty scope and class scopes two general groups of additional layout scopes exist. *slot hiding scopes* only give access to a part of the actually declared slots, and *slot issuing scopes* give access to more slots than are declared by the scope. The following two examples both introduce new slots and thus are to be seen as slot issuing scopes.

5.3.1 Bit Field Layout Scope

In several languages the number of instances variables is restricted, for instance many Smalltalk VMs limit the number of instances variables to something less than 64 on many systems. When using many instance variables that only use booleans it feels natural to combine them into a single field. Normally each instance variable would require a full pointer to store a value that can be represented with a single bit. Combining these variables into a single field helps to reduce the memory footprint of an object. In our implementation we can combine multiple boolean fields into a single bit field. This not only reduces the memory footprint but also helps to speed up the garbage collection. Due to the single field the garbage collector has to traverse fewer fields.

Listing 5.7 shows the implementation of the `BitSlot`. Each `BitSlot` knows its storage location in the object denoted by the `bitSlot` instance variable. The `bitIndex` is used to extract the corresponding bit out of the integer stored at the location of the `bitSlot`. In order to read a boolean value, the `BitSlot` reads the full integer value from the `bitSlot` and masks out the corresponding bit.

```
VirtualSlot subclass: #BitSlot
    layout: PointerLayout
    slots: {
        #bitIndex     => PositiveIntegerSlot.
        #bitFieldSlot => TypedSlot type: BitHolderSlot.
    }

read: anInstance
    mask ← (0x01 >> index).
    ↑ (bitFieldSlot read: anInstance) & mask == mask.

write: aBoolean to: anInstance
    |int|
    int ← bitFieldSlot read: anInstance.
    int ← int & (0x01 >> index) invert.    "mask the bit"
    int ← int | (aBoolean asBit >> index)  "set the bit"
    bitSlot write: int to: anInstance
    ↑ aBoolean
```

Listing 5.7: Bit Field Slot Implementation

Using bit fields in a normal object is a matter of changing the slot definition. Instead of using the default `Slot` the `BitSlot` has to be used. Listing 5.8 shows the basic definition of an object using bit slots. When using such an object up to 30 bit slots are combined into a single field. Figure 5.4 shows a transcript of how the boolean values are written to the single instance variable. If this were implemented without encapsulating the behavior in slots, the code of the `write:to:` or `read:` method would have to be copied at least into a getter or setter. In this case there is a single definition of the extraction semantics in the bit slot, which serves as a template.

```
Object subclass: #BitObject
    layout: PointerLayout
    slots: {
        boolean1 => BitSlot.
        boolean2 => BitSlot.
            ...
        booleanN => BitSlot.
    }
```

Listing 5.8: Bit Object using Bit Slots

Unlike the previous examples of slots the `BitSlots` require the layout to add a storage slot. As a reminder, the `BitSlots` are virtual and hence do not occupy a field in the instance. The situation is further complicated in that the number of storage slots is not fixed and depends on the number

5.3. First-Class Layout Scopes

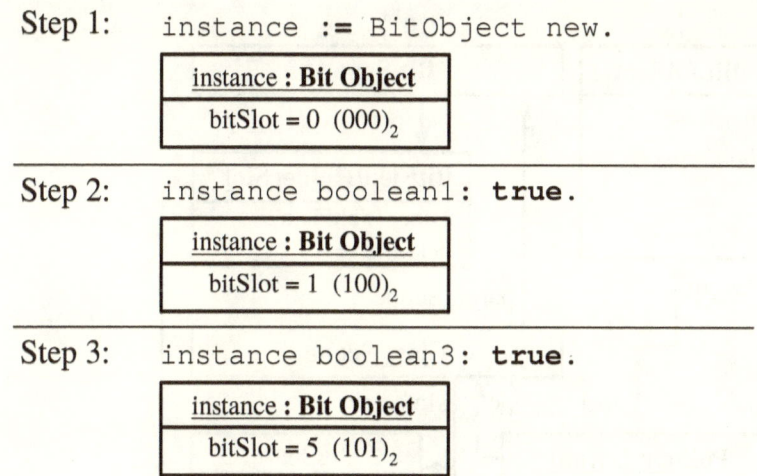

Figure 5.4: A BitField Instance in Action

of `BitSlots`, since each storage integer has a fixed number of bits. Instead of changing the current class scope, and thus obfuscating the original slots definition we add specific bit scopes. In Figure 5.5 we see that the layout of the `Bit Object` points to a normal class scope which contains the slot definition mentioned in the class definition. Instead of linking directly to the class scope defining the slots of the superclass the parent scope is set to a special bit field scope. The bit scope internally contains the bit slot which is used to store the different bits in it. Each virtual bit slot points to a non-virtual bit field slot defined in a bit scope.

5.3.2 Property Layout Scope

The previous example using bit fields displayed that by using slots and slots scopes it is possible to transparently optimize the footprint of an object using boolean instance variables. Here we will show how this technique can be used to selectively but drastically transform the layout of objects.

JavaScript [59] and Python [119] use dictionaries as the internal representation for objects. This enables the dynamic addition of instance variables and saves memory when there are many unused instance variables. The simplicity of the object design comes with two major drawbacks however: 1) typing mistakes in instance variable names are not easily detected, and 2) attribute access is difficult to optimize.

In standard Smalltalk the number of instance variables is fixed up-front in the class. However we easily overcome this limitation by using an intermediate dictionary which holds all the object's instance variables. Without first-class layouts this would force us to use unchecked symbols as field names to access the properties. Furthermore each instance variable access

69

Chapter 5. First-Class Object Layouts

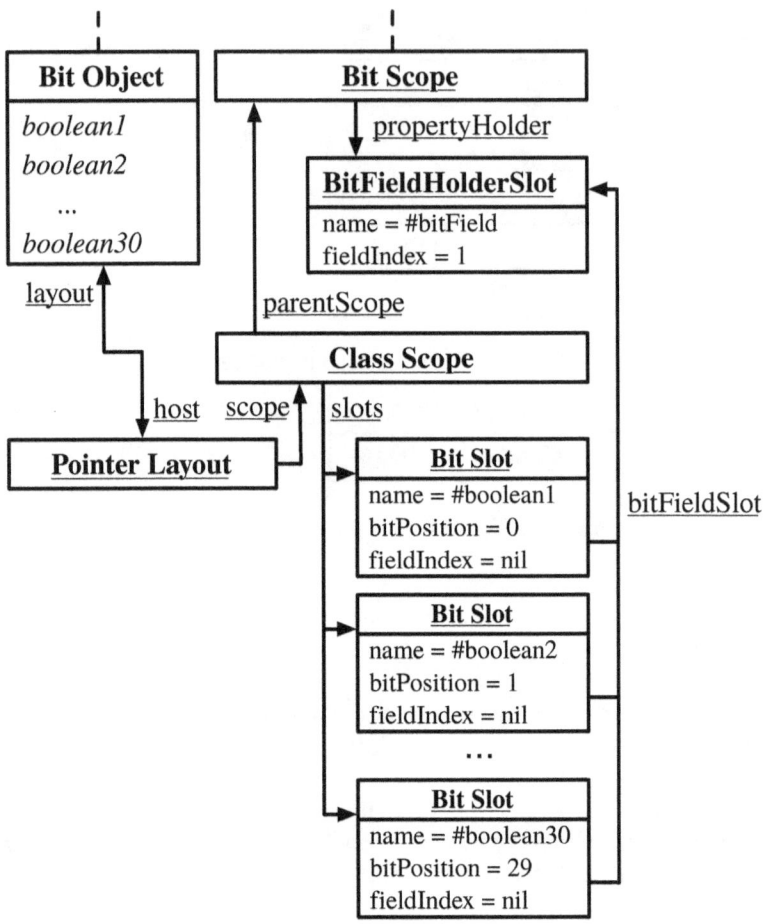

Figure 5.5: Bit Field Scope Example

would have to be manually replaced with a dictionary access, which can be completely avoided in our case. In our implementation it is possible to benefit from both worlds by only enabling dictionary-based storage where it is needed, while still providing syntax checking for slots.

```
Object subclass: #PropertyObject
    layout: PointerLayout
    slots: {
        field     => Slot
        property1 => PropertySlot.
        property2 => PropertySlot.
             ...
        propertyN => PropertySlot.
    }
```

5.3. First-Class Layout Scopes

Listing 5.9: Property Object using Property Slots

Listing 5.9 provides a class definition of an object which uses a normal slot, named `field` and an arbitrary number of virtual slots that use a dictionary as storage target. Figure 5.6 shows an example usage of this property object. Note that the resulting instance uses only two fields. The property holder named `dict` is lazily filled with the values for the different properties.

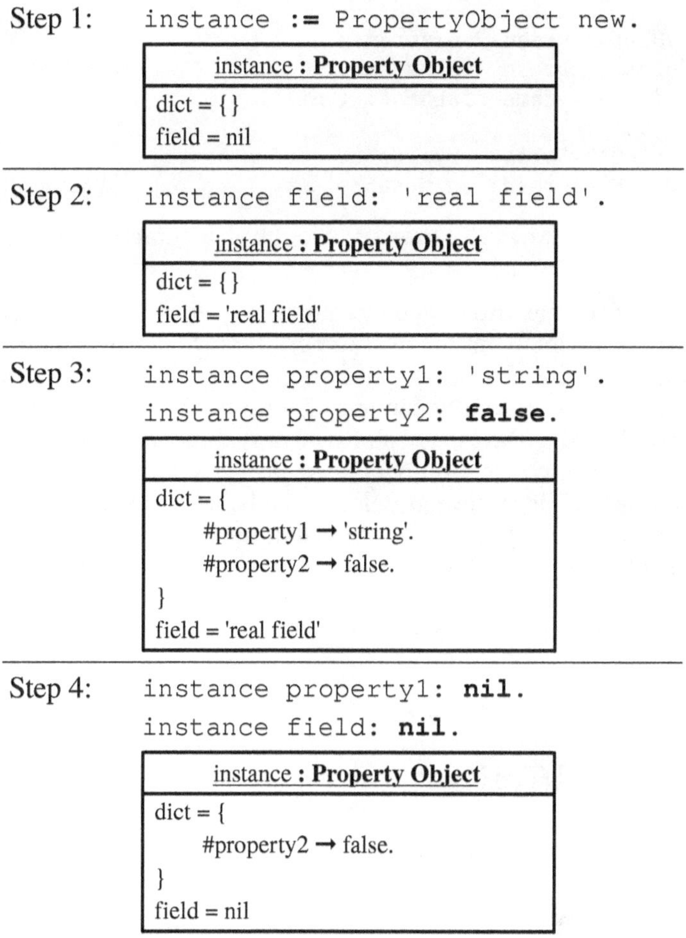

Step 1:   `instance := PropertyObject new.`

instance : **Property Object**
dict = { }
field = nil

Step 2:   `instance field: 'real field'.`

instance : **Property Object**
dict = { }
field = 'real field'

Step 3:   `instance property1: 'string'.`
               `instance property2: `**`false.`**

instance : **Property Object**

dict = {
     #property1 → 'string'.
     #property2 → false.
 }
 field = 'real field'

Step 4:   `instance property1: `**`nil.`**
               `instance field: `**`nil.`**

instance : **Property Object**

dict = {
     #property2 → false.
 }
 field = nil

Figure 5.6: Property Object in Action

Similar to the previous bit field example we have to introduce a data holder slot depending on the types of specified slot. In this case we use a special property scope. Figure 5.7 shows that the property scope holds an instance of the `PropertyHolderSlot` class which is required to reserve one field for the property storage. This field holds a *property dictionary* that maps *property slots* onto their values. Listing 5.10 shows how accesses are rewritten by property slots so that they access the state via the property dictionary.

```
VirtualSlot subclass: #PropertySlot
    layout: PointerLayout
    slots: {
        #dictSlot => TypedSlot type: PropertyHolderSlot.
    }.

PropertySlot >> read: anInstance
    ↑ (dictSlot read: anInstance)
            at: name ifAbsent: [ nil ].

PropertySlot >> write: aValue to: anInstance
    ↑ (dictSlot read: anInstance) at: name put: aValue.
```

Listing 5.10: Property Slot Implementation

This approach has three main advantages over the default behavior in Python or JavaScript. First the overall performance of the system does not suffer since only the accesses of selected property slots are rewritten to go over the dictionary. Secondly converting a property slot into a normal slot is matter of changing the type of slot. The only difficulty is that special care has to be taken to convert the values in property dictionaries of existing live instances back into normal fields. Finally, in contrast to the standard Python or JavaScript approach our model minimizes the risk of runtime errors related to misspelled variable names by requiring the property slots to be explicitly specified in the layout scope up-front. This allows us to provide proper compile-time checks of property slots just like for all other Smalltalk slots.

5.4 Stateful Traits

In this section we show that by reifying the state of the objects and making it available in the programming language new language features that revolve around state can be implemented with less effort. As case-study we implement stateful traits [49], a mechanism for sharing behavior and state in standard object-oriented systems which is orthogonal to subclassing. Stateful traits are components of reuse that are more fine-grained than classes but generally larger than slots.

Although a previous implementation for Smalltalk exists it was more difficult to attain and includes ad-hoc solutions like renaming instance variables to avoid name clashes.

5.4. Stateful Traits

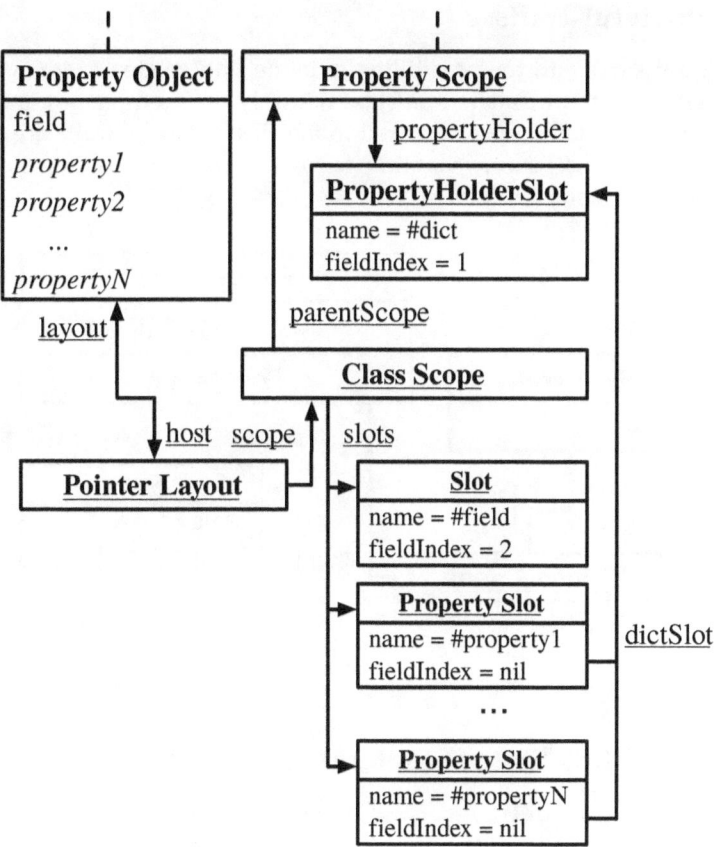

Figure 5.7: Property Scope Example

5.4.1 Traits

Fundamentally traits are used as collections of reusable methods that are installed on classes. Normally, installing a trait is implemented by flattening out the collection in the method dictionary of the target class. All conflicts resulting from installing a trait have to be resolved by the developer. This includes renaming methods, rejecting methods and overriding methods.

Before installation the trait object is copied. The trait methods are recompiled on the receiving class to ensure correct semantics for superclass sends. Whenever a trait-related method is modified, the trait and all its users are notified of the change and updated accordingly. A trait is uninstalled by removing all methods introduced by the trait. Finally whenever a class is updated, its trait composition is copied over from the previous version of the class to the new version of the class.

5.4.2 Stateful Traits

Stateful traits [10] add the possibility to define state related to traits. When composing a stateful trait with a class not only the methods are installed, but also the associated state is added to the class. Stateful traits are closely related to mixins [22] except that they follow the conflict-avoiding composition strategy of standard traits.

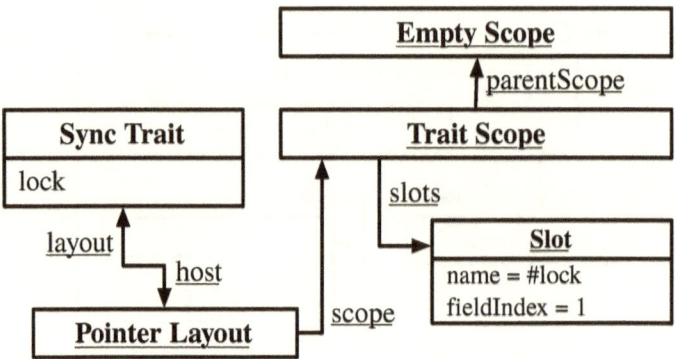

Figure 5.8: Stateful Trait Example

5.4.3 Installing State of Stateful Traits

By relying on our model of first-class layouts and scopes it becomes straightforward to extend traits with state. A stateful trait is in essence a subclass of Trait which is extended with a layout. Where we previously declared a class to use a trait, we can now allow it to equally rely on a stateful trait. The behavior has to be mixed in at the exact same location as standard traits. The only additional step required is the mixing of the state declared by the trait with the state declared by the class. Figure 5.8 shows an example of such a stateful trait, the Sync Trait. In addition to the provided methods, the stateful trait has a layout. This layout is linked to the related *trait scope* which contains a single slot lock.

The class builder is the tool responsible for installing the state of a stateful trait. During this process we want to avoid name clashes with the state of the target class. To avoid complex renaming required by the original stateful trait work, we introduce a new kind of layout scope in our model, the *fork scope*. A fork scope is a scope that does not only have a parent scope, just like a normal class scope, but also a list of side scopes. The side scopes contribute to the final number of fields that an associated object has, but they do not provide any visible slots. Their state in the resulting object is essentially private to the owner of the scope. The trait scopes are then installed in the fork scope as side scopes. Figure 5.9 shows how the trait from Figure 5.8 is applied to the Sync Stream class.

5.4. Stateful Traits

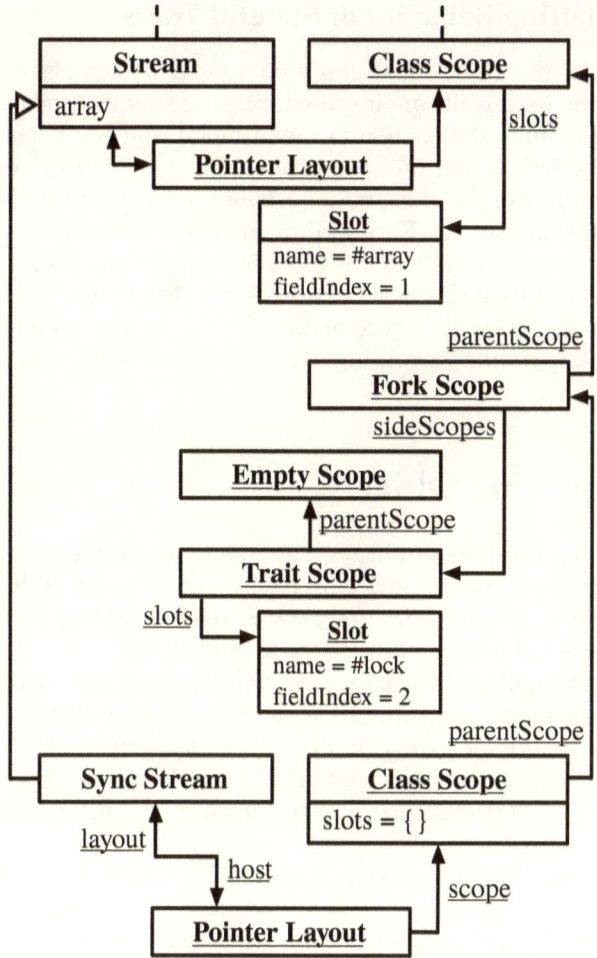

Figure 5.9: Stateful Trait with Fork Scopes

The modelling challenge when installing stateful traits is to correctly update the field indices and scope instance variable access. The index calculation has to take into account the fields in the superclass and other installed traits.

For the normal operations on a class (*e.g.*, compiling a method inside the class) the visible slots will be computed by recursively traversing the parent links of the scopes, aggregating the slots from the class scopes, but ignoring the side scopes of fork scopes. During compilation of the trait-specific behavior the trait providing the behavior is used as a compilation target. This way, at compilation time, the class methods do not have access to the trait state and vice-versa.

5.4.4 Installing Behavior of Stateful Traits

After the class has been successfully composed by the class builder, the methods of the used traits are installed. Stateful trait methods are installed by updating them in the context of the installed trait copy, meaning in the context of the trait scope that was installed rather than the original trait scope. The indices of the slots in the installed scope are already updated to reflect their installed offset. Recompiling methods in the installed scope will equally update them to reflect this modification. This is a simplification of the *copy down* technique [6] in that it does not try to save memory but always installs methods by copy. Bytecode modification can be used to reduce the cost of installing traits by avoiding full compilation of the trait methods for each use.

5.5 Inspecting Objects

The objects in a run-time application are the main source of debugging information. For this reason Smalltalk environments come with a variety of object inspectors. These inspectors allow developers to look at objects using the structural meta-information retrieved from classes.

Given that Smalltalk normally only provides the class structure and instance variable names as information about the state of objects, basic object inspectors only provide a very limited way of looking at objects. They render the object as a list of instance variable to field value associations. The inspectors often implement mechanisms to easily navigate from one object to the objects it contains.

More advanced inspectors rely on a metaobject protocol to retrieve meta-information about instances. They allow classes to specialize the view on their instances by customizing the methods used by the inspector. This mechanism only directly supports a very coarse-grained specialization: If an object requires different views for the different instance variables, its class has to implement its own infrastructure to support this. This is useful for example for rendering hash tables as key-value pairs rather rather than the internal structure used to optimally store the values.

Layouts, scopes, and slots not only provide a natural extension point for behavior in relation to structure, but since they declare the structure of objects they offer an ideal back-end to provide information about instances. Rather than fully implementing the metaobject protocol for inspecting directly on the class, the class forwards it to the layout metaobject. This object relies on the scopes to get extra information about the structure, and slots to retrieve information about the instance variables. This provides fine-grained control for the rendering of instances to the relevant classes, and thus eases reuse of code related to the inspecting. At the same time the protocol is separated from the class instance and thus provides proper stratification as required by mirror-based reflection (see subsection 3.1.2).

The protocol for inspecting is especially important in combination with custom structural metaobjects. Since for example bit fields, as described in subsection 5.3.1, merge multiple slots into a single field, traditional inspectors would not provide proper insight into the structure of the instance. The merged values would be displayed as they are in memory, rather than rendering their higher-level meaning.

5.6 Dynamic Structure Modifications

Dynamically updating software, *e.g.*, for developing and debugging the system without restarting it, has long been common practice in dynamic object-oriented languages such as JavaScript, Ruby, Smalltalk, *etc.* Despite their popularity and long history, dynamic software updates remain challenging. Changes such as removing and adding an instance variable can be challenging because it is unclear what should happen to the instances of the changed class. Changing the order of instance variables can be challenging, because while the semantics are clear, a possibly large number of methods is affected. In both cases, a high-level, structural change entails a number of changes on a much lower level.

In this section we propose models that capture structural changes both from a high-level language point of view, as well as a low-level implementation view. Modifications to the layout are captured in a *class modification model* and refined into two *field modification models*, a *method modification model* and an *instance modification model*. We show how these abstractions can ease previously messy tasks, such as dealing with structural changes, and implementing appropriate responses to those changes.

5.6.1 Modification Model

Modification models capture changes to layouts and simplify the propagation of these changes to other impacted elements of the system. Figure 5.10 shows the main classes of the modification model and how they relate to layouts and slots. Following the previously argued necessity to split between high-level and low-level details, our model is comprised of class modifications (high-level) that can be refined into field modifications (low-level).

Class modification. A class modification captures the structural changes to a class at the slot level. A class modification is computed out of two versions of a class layout and contains separate lists of slots that have been added, removed, modified, and left untouched. Modifications to a class can impact its subclasses. As a consequence, a class modification can have so-called class modification *propagations*, which model changes performed to all subclasses.

Chapter 5. First-Class Object Layouts

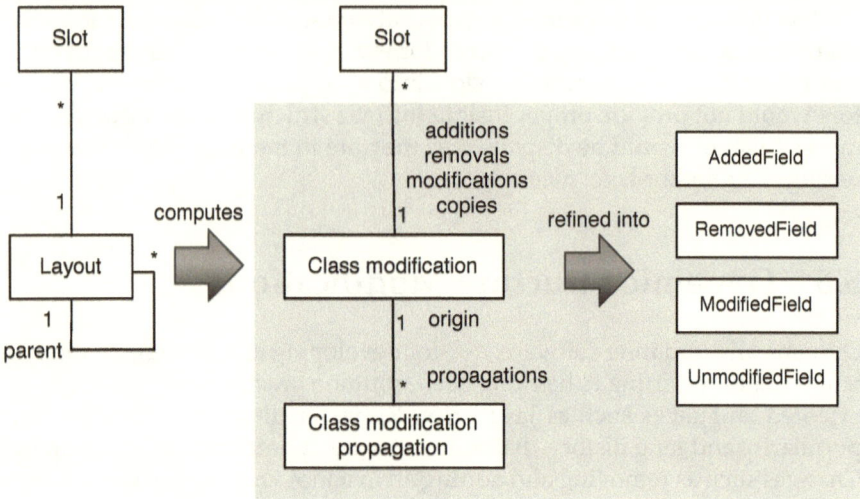

Figure 5.10: Main classes in the modification model and how they relate to the other abstractions

Low-level modifications. Modifications to a high-level class have an impact on the related low-level structures. There are two modification models that transform the high-level model into concrete low-level modifications models, the *method modification model* and the *instance modification model*. Both models list for every field, whether it was added, removed, or shifted to a new position.

The instance modification model maps new positions onto old ones. This allows the instance migration mechanism to easily initialize new instances from old ones, automatically disregarding discarded state (there is no new state mapping to old state that is discarded).

The method modification model maps old positions to new ones. This allows a code rewriter to update existing accesses to fields by replacing old indices with new indices. In case the user has not provided custom slots or layouts, the system-provided slots act as follows. (1) If a field was shifted, all accesses to those fields are modified accordingly. (2) If a field was removed, all accesses to that field are replaced by a special native code sequence that the compiler does not otherwise create, to mark an illegal field access. If it is executed, it raises a run-time exception.

5.6.2 Building and Installing

The specified modifications are carried out by informing the rest of the system of the change, and by applying the transformations in the instance and method modification model. In our approach, the responsibility to carry out the modifications lies with two main components: the class builder and a class installer.

Class builder. The class builder is responsible for the structural part of modifying a class or creating a new class. It relies on the installer to fetch the old version of the class. It then uses the class modification model to compute the method modification and instance modification models. It then validates that these changes are semantically sound.

Class installer. Once the class builder has correctly built and validated a modification model, a class installer is responsible for transactionally[5] installing the change into the system. The class installer is the interface between the class building process and the rest of the live system.[6] Our system provides an abstract class installer that has to be specialized with a specific installation strategy that knows which subsystems to notify of changes, how to migrate live instances, and how to update existing methods. This allows different installers to implement different strategies to deal with the update of impacted method code, and with the migration of the instances of the impacted classes.

5.6.3 Pharo Class Installer

When a class is structurally changed in Pharo, the Pharo class installer migrates all instances and updates the methods of the class and its subclasses to reflect the structural change. It does not, however, update any running threads that might be affected by the change. We reimplemented the Pharo installer as an extension to our abstract class installer so that it relies on the modification models. This greatly simplifies the installer since almost all the behavior is already captured by our abstract class installer.

The resulting installer first updates all methods of the old versions of the classes to adapt to the new versions of the classes. It relies on a *method field updater* to apply the changes using the method modification model. The method field updater decompiles[7] the bytecodes of the methods to a slightly higher-level IR (intermediate representation), updates the field accesses and compiles the IR back to bytecode. This saves a complete trip through all the phases of the compilation process, including parsing.

During this process the field accesses occurring in the IR are linked back to the field modification models. These modification models know which slots are related to the particular field. There may be at most one slot of each

---

[5]The installer must modify the classes and migrate all instances without other code handling the related instances or classes. Otherwise the resulting runtime might end up in an inconsistent state, possibly containing multiple versions of a single class or instance.

[6]Note that our model does not include a mechanism for migrating already running threads to the new version of the classes. This is the responsibility of more complex dynamic software update mechanisms that rely on our model—which are yet to be implemented.

[7]We built the decompiler for this project, and made it available as part of the OPAL compiler package. http://www.squeaksource.com/OpalCompiler.html

the old version and the new version. This allows the slots to coordinate the updating of field accesses.

The installer then migrates live instances by creating new instances of the new versions of the modified classes from the existing instances. The installer implements instance migration by relying on instance modification models. After migrating the instances, it migrates the old versions of the classes to the new versions. Both instance migration and class migration happen in one single *stop-the-world* transaction.

5.6.4 Metrics

The original Pharo class builder takes a naive approach to updating bytecodes to a changed class structure: it recompiles all methods of the class. We replaced the original Pharo class builder by our own class builder. Our class builder makes use of the method modification model. This allowed us to experiment with language changes, and let us estimate the increase in code size that using method modification models entails.

The overall code size of our replacement of the class builder, including all models, is 2109 lines of code. Out of this, 1194 lines of code form the new class builder[8]. The size of the original Pharo class builder[9] is 1092 lines of code. Thus, the amount of code increased by a factor of 1.9, for the whole model, and for the mere class building, by a factor of 1.1.

The increase in complexity is compensated by a significant gain in flexibility. It also buys a significant performance gain in recompiling classes. The process of 10 times adding and immediately removing again an instance variable to a class with 14 subclasses was sped up from 31.2 to 4.6 seconds[10], leading to a speedup by factor 6.8. On a class with no subclasses, nor any installed methods, the same procedure took 1.2 seconds on both the default Pharo class builder and in our system. We conclude that our implementation combines higher flexibility and a clearer design with performance that is at worst as fast, and at times 6.8 times faster than the naive implementation.

5.7 Related Work

Various techniques in software engineering exist to to address problems that stem from the lack of appropriate programming language abstractions. In this section we list several techniques whose *raison d'être* is, at least partially, to address the lack of adequate abstractions for object state manipulation, access, and composition.

---

[8]In build 229 of our system, http://www.squeaksource.com/PlayOut.html

[9]As ships in version 1.2.1 final of Pharo Smalltalk.

[10]All measurements were performed on a 2011 MacBook pro at 2.3 GHz. We used the Cog virtual machine, build VM.r2378. The transformed class is RBProgramNode, as contained in Pharo 1.2.1 final.

5.7.1 Language Extensions

When application concerns cannot be properly expressed in a programming language, this leads to crosscutting boilerplate code. External DSLs [76, 63] are often used to address this problem. When external DSLs are tightly integrated into our programming language they essentially become language extensions [101, 122]. However, application-specific extensions to a language limit understandability, usability and portability.

Mixins [22] and traits [49, 10] are language extensions built for reuse below the class-level. They promote removal of boilerplate code by extracting it to the introduced reusable components. Traits improve over mixins by requiring explicit conflict resolution and avoiding lookup problems resulting from multiple inheritance through the flattening property. While both approaches support reuse related to the state of objects, the abstractions themselves are fairly heavy-weight and they require *glue code*, another form of boilerplate code, to configure the final class.

Aspect-oriented programming [87], a language extension in itself, addresses the problem of cross-cutting concerns related to behaviour in a system. Nevertheless, it does not address the cross-cutting problems regarding state.

5.7.2 Meta Modeling

As opposed to language extensions, meta modeling focuses on describing data by relying on existing language features. These meta descriptions do not interfere with the core language and thus are decoupled from the actual objects they describe. However, if an application solely accesses the attributes of its instances through first-class meta-descriptions, these meta-descriptions provide an interface to customize the semantics of state access.

Magritte [121] is a meta modelling framework mainly used together with Seaside [11]. Magritte is used to describe attributes, relationships and their constraints. All descriptions are provided as first-class Smalltalk objects. Magritte provides a complete interface to read and write attributes of an instance through its meta descriptions. A favorable property of Magritte is, that its meta-descriptions are described in terms of themselves. This way it is possible to rely on the same tools to work with instances and with the model themselves.

Magritte, and meta-modelling tools in general, overlap in many regions with our approach of first-class layouts, scopes, and slots. However, these tools are built on top of an existing language and not embedded into it. Magritte's meta-description are decoupled from the classes of an object. Hence, the objects themselves do not directly benefit from their added meta-descriptions. Smalltalk code is not obliged to use the meta-descriptions. It can directly access instance variables of the receiver, and assign values which conflict with the well-defined meta-description. Thus, meta-modelling frameworks show only the same behavior as first-class slots when attributes of objects are accessed solely through the meta-descriptions. But due to the decoupled implementation, this is not enforced and rather relies on the discipline of the programmer.

5.7.3 Annotations

Several programming languages support annotations to attach metadata to program structure. Java annotations, available since version 5.0 of the language, are probably the most prominent example. Annotations are generally a way to directly attach meta information to source elements. Later on the information in the annotations can be queried using a reflection API. In this sense annotations cannot be used directly to alter state access. However it is possible to provide new tools which use annotations to control access and validate the state of a model. In Java, annotations can be supplied for classes, methods and instance variables. Generally the annotations are only used for adding meta-descriptions to the code. This metadata is then later accessed at runtime using reflection. Example use-cases of annotations include unit-tests [8] and compile-time model verification [57].

Annotations can be used to avoid manually writing boilerplate code by generating code from the annotations. Java 6 features pluggable annotation processors that can hook into the compiler and transform the AST. However it is not possible to directly modify the annotated sources. Using this infrastructure it is only possible to create new class definitions that take slot definitions into account. Due to this limitation it would be required to use the generated sources.

5.7.4 Object Relational Mapping

A special case of meta modelling worth mentioning is the use of structural and semantic meta information to model object relational mapping [7]. Meta information is needed to provide a meaningful mapping from the objects to the database. However generally the objects should stay fully functional thus some part of the semantics described in the meta information has to be available.

Several object oriented front ends for relational databases support slot-like structures to describe the database fields. Django [43] provides several types of fields to describe and constrain what kind of data can be stored in the different instance variables. This metadata is further used to create the table description. Although the field descriptors could be directly used to generate getters and setters which dynamically validate the assigned data, this is only done when serializing the object to the database. As such relationships are only indirectly usable by storing and loading objects from the database.

In the Active Record implementation used with Ruby on Rails class-side methods are used to create descriptions of the fields used in a table. These methods use Ruby's reflective capabilities to install getters and setters. In this sense there are no slot objects but class-side methods to create slot descriptions.

5.7.5 First-Class Slots

The Common Lisp Object System (CLOS) [16, 112] provides support for first-class slots[11]. Upon defining a class slots are described as part of the class definition. Internally CLOS uses this information to decide which slot class to use. Standard CLOS always relies on the default slot class. In Persistent CLOS (PCLOS) [111] the lookup was customized, to decide based on an extra keyword whether the default or the persistent slot class should be used. On accessing slots the slot-value function is called. This is a generic function similar to the instVarAt: and instVarAt:put: methods in Smalltalk which can be used to directly access the fields of an object using indices. It can be overridden to specialize slot access for the entire class. Internally this function relies on a class-side method slot-value-using-class. This method can finally specialize variable access to the type of class and the type of slot.

While CLOS already provides slots as one of the main reifications, standard CLOS does not provide a way to specialize instance variable access. As PCLOS shows it would however be fairly easy to hook into the protocol and allow programmers to provide custom slot metaobjects. CLOS however does not reify any instance structure beyond the level of slots.

The E programming language [135] provides slots as objects representing the location where values of instance variables are stored for specific instances. This model is the closest to what is presented in this chapter. However it requires the system to generate a multitude of objects for each user-level object, as all instance variables of a single instance need their own metaobject.

C and C++ provide references which can be used to mimic the availability of first-class slots. However such references are simply *lvalues* providing direct access to the raw memory. They cannot influence any access semantics, nor do they provide a higher-level abstraction that can be reused by other instance variables by bundling accessor methods.

5.7.6 Unified Slots and Methods

In Self [142] and Newspeak [21] message sends and slot access are unified. In Self everything is a slot access, so methods are just special slots that require dynamic calculation. The opposite view is that slots are just special methods that retrieve their value from memory. This forces the user to always access values through a standardized interface that can flexibly react

---

[11]What we call fields is called slots in CLOS. Slot is named slot-descriptor in CLOS.

to change. Even more interesting is that objects can specialize the inherited slots through overriding, just like inherited methods. Data becomes completely public since slots cannot be hidden. Since the accessors and initialization code have to be overridden separately, this implies that they have to be specialized over and over again for each individual slot. There is no standard way to bundle these methods in a specialized metaobject and install them as a single unit.

5.7.7 Dynamic Software Update

Techniques to dynamically update production systems have been the subject of intensive research [137, 73, 96]. The emphasis in this case is on ensuring *program correctness* before and after the roll-out of the update, which requires well-timed migration of data [130]. Works in the field of dynamic updates focus on what constraints the migration should comply to and low-level implementation details, and not on the design of consistent and extensible language mechanisms to better support changes at run-time [109]. The problem of evolving object instances (sometimes called long-lived objects, or persistent objects) has been studied in the object-oriented database community [20, 114].

Change-oriented development [125, 108, 51] aims at tracking and enabling changes in software with fine-grained change models. The goal of these models is to provide better insights into the nature of software development and provide better user experiences in IDEs. Our goal is different and we aim at supporting dynamic evolution with a modification model that abstracts low-level details and provides higher-level abstractions that can be extended. Penn *et al.* [114] provide a classification of all possible software changes. Our prototype supports all changes they list.

Dynamic software updating is a cross-disciplinary research topic that covers software-engineering, programming language design, and operating systems [96, 110, 137, 130, 73, 31, 107]. The challenge to provide developers with a simple programming model that is practical—safe, efficient, and that allows developers to easily specify the necessary custom migration logic— is still open. Reflection has traditionally been used to provide means for run-time adaptations [124]. It is however orthogonal to safety, and it is then also a challenge to extend the reflective architecture so as to support safe dynamic updates.

5.8 Summary

The lack of proper abstractions to reify object state is often the reason for the introduction of boilerplate code. To address this problem, in this chapter we proposed to extend the structural reflective model of the language with *object layouts*, *layout scopes* and *slots*. Layouts and slots are first-class building blocks encapsulating the assumptions that conventionally exist only as implicit contracts between the virtual machine and the compiler. Layouts describe the object layout of instances of a class while slots represent the conceptual link between instance variables and fields. Layout scopes reify how classes extend the layout of their superclass.

We have shown

- that first-class slots encapsulate the definition of custom semantics for instance variable *initialization*, *access* and *migration* (*e.g.*, first-class relationships), promoting consistent fine-grained reuse,
- that layout scopes support language extensions (*e.g.*, stateful traits) that influence layout composition,
- and that a customizable class installer provides a framework for building dynamic software update mechanisms.

We have classified slots into *primitive slots*, *customized slots* and *virtual slots* and provided examples for each. The programming language tool that requires the most fundamental change to support our layout-based model is the class builder, and we have shown how even its implementation becomes simpler by using slots.

In Chapter 4 we introduced messaging as a first-class building block for interaction between objects. In this chapter we complemented that model with object layouts, layout scopes and slots as first-class building blocks for the objects themselves. In following chapter, we avoid the need to bridge the gap between debuggers and the execution format by making the behavior of applications first-class. We provide access to the semantics of execution within one object by storing the AST nodes of methods, and providing access to first-class interpreters for those AST nodes.

Chapter 5. First-Class Object Layouts

6

First-Class Interpreters

In Section 3.3 we argued that VMs are closed for extension. As a consequence, in Chapter 4 we eliminated the VM by translating Smalltalk code to native code supported by a metacircular runtime library. Nevertheless, debuggers and language experiments are often more conveniently implemented by modifying the interpreter of a language [140]. In this chapter we show how Pinocchio supports language experimentation and debugging, without support from an underlying runtime implementation, by supporting first-class interpreters.

The Pinocchio compiler stores a complete reflective model of the application code, including a secondary representation of methods using the AST nodes [36]. The semantics of Pinocchio are reified as a first-class AST interpreter. Applications specify their own interpreters *inside* the runtime as subclasses of this default `Interpreter` class. Applications freely flow from interpreter to interpreter depending on the required semantics.

The contributions of this chapter are:

- a novel approach to behavioral reflection inspired by Refci's first-class interpreters [133];
- the design and implementation of a proof-of-concept prototype of the approach;
- the presentation of three non-trivial case studies demonstrating how first-class interpreters facilitate behavioral reflection.

The prototype of first-class interpreters is implemented in an older version of Pinocchio than described in Chapter 4. This particular version relies on bytecode interpretation of Smalltalk code, rather than native compilation. However, other than general speedup from a faster runtime, all the concepts explained in this chapter also apply in the natively compiled version. Nevertheless, it is important to notice that in Chapter 4 the meta-level and base-level are conflated. This is due to the overlap between invoking the meta-level `invoke:`, and invoking inline cached methods. As motivated in subsection 3.1.2, to avoid confusion meta-levels should be clearly separated. This implies that meta-level code, such as the `invoke:` method, should execute at the meta-level of the first-class interpreter, while other code runs at the base-level of (on top of) the first-class interpreter.

Outline In Section 6.1 we present first-class interpreters in a nutshell, and we explain how custom interpreters are built and subsequently used. Section 6.2 illustrates how a first-class interpreter can easily be extended to support debugging, and then motivates the design of multiple interpreters with the help of an example of a specialized interpreter to support object-flow analysis for back-in-time debugging and a parallel debugger. Section 6.4 compares Pinocchio to other dynamic languages in terms of performance, and outlines the further steps required to turn Pinocchio into a fast approach to behavioral reflection. Section 6.6 concludes with a brief summary of the results.

6.1 First-Class Interpreters in a Nutshell

Pinocchio enables lightweight language experimentation and debugging using first-class interpreters. It provides a default `Interpreter` class that defines a meta-circular interpreter implemented as an AST visitor. It reuses and exploits three features from Smalltalk for light-weight extensibility:

- *the object model:* interpreters adopt the object model of Smalltalk— since specialized interpreters typically make only modest changes to their base-level semantics, objects can often flow freely between levels;

- *recursion:* interpreters are defined as recursive AST visitors instead of as bytecode interpreters with explicit stacks — first-class continuations can be used to implement non-local flow of control;

- *garbage collection:* interpreters can rely on the garbage collection provided by their meta-level.

Behavioral reflection is supported by explicitly instantiating first-class interpreters that subclass the default interpreter. Extending interpreters is facilitated by the fact that AST nodes are semantically closer to the original source code than bytecode [37, 42]. This also implies that tools relying on first-class interpreters are portable across platforms.

To construct a new variant of the Pinocchio interpreter it suffices to subclass the Interpreter class and override a part of its interface (see Figure 6.1).

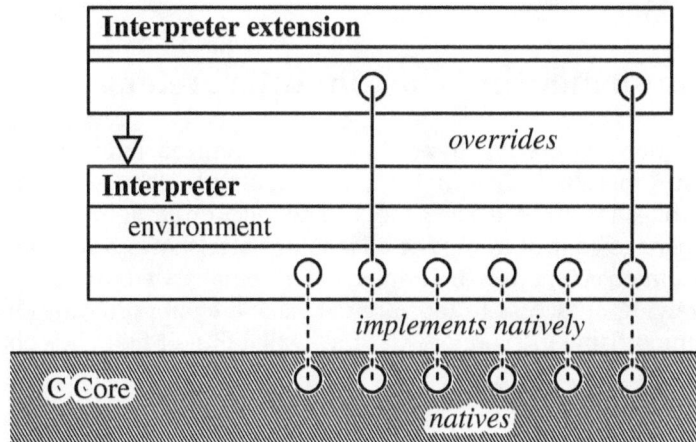

Figure 6.1: Native methods in the Interpreter and interpreter extension through subclassing

The interpretation of an application is altered simply by passing the application in the form of a closure to a customized interpreter. For example, the expression

```
Debugger interpret: [ self runApplication ].
```

will cause the passed closure [self runApplication] to be evaluated by the Debugger interpreter.

As usual, closures encapsulate an *environment* and an *expression* object. When starting up a specialized interpreter, the continuation of the interpreted application is empty. The interpreter installs the enclosed environment and starts evaluating the expression in this environment. Since the passed expression for the default interpreter is a closure, it is evaluated by sending the message value to the closure on top of the interpreter:

```
interpret: aClosure
    ↑ self send: (Message new selector: #value)
            to: aClosure.
```

Although it might seem correct to directly evaluate the closure by invoking aClosure value, this is incorrect as the closure would be evaluated at the wrong level of interpretation. It would run at the level of the custom interpreter (the meta-level from the application's point-of-view) rather than on top of the interpreter as desired.

The open design of the meta-circular interpreter lets programmers extend the runtime with very little effort. More importantly, the extensions to the interpreter are implemented within the language provided by the runtime itself. As such they can be implemented using any of the existing tools for the language, including development environments, debuggers, test-runners and versioning systems.

6.2 Implementing Custom Interpreters

In this section we present three different customized interpreters implemented in Pinocchio[1]. We first introduce a simple debugger that reuses garbage collection and the object model, and relies on straightforward recursion to manage control flow. The alias interpreter shows how interpreters with custom object models are implemented. Finally we outline how interpreters relying on access to the runtime stack are supported in Pinocchio through modifiable interpreters and the availability of first-class continuations.

6.2.1 A Simple Debugger

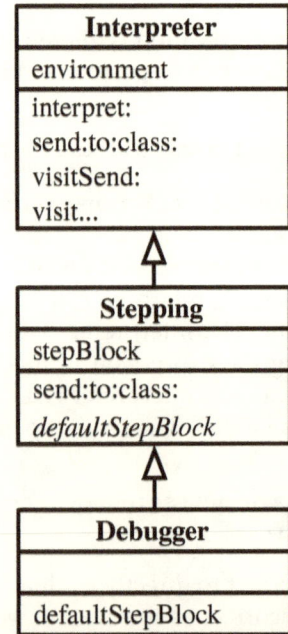

Figure 6.2: Specializing a meta-circular interpreter

---

[1]The full sources of these use cases are available under http://scg.unibe.ch/download/pinocchio/pinocchio_svn1397_mc196.zip.

To show how extensions to existing interpreters are implemented and used we first describe the implementation of a simple debugger. It executes a program while allowing the user to pause evaluation at the level of message sends. In order to start evaluating code using a debugger, the user passes the code to the debugger in the form of a closure:

```
Debugger interpret:  [ self runApplication ].
```

The debugger takes control over the evaluation of the block. At each message send it allows the user to decide to step to the next message send, to inspect the current receiver, to step over the evaluation of the message send or to evaluate Pinocchio statements. This is a typical subset of actions available in any debugger.

As shown in Figure 6.2, to implement the debugger in Pinocchio, we start by creating the stepping interpreter class as a subclass of the standard `Interpreter`. The stepping interpreter overrides the methods in charge of evaluating message sends. Rather than directly executing a send, the stepping interpreter delays this behavior and first gives control to a `stepBlock` installed on the interpreter instance:

```
send: message to: receiver class: class
   ↑ stepBlock value: receiver
               value: class
               value: message
               value: [ super
                         send: message
                         to: receiver
                         class: class ].
```

The `stepBlock` of the interpreter can be used to flexibly modify the message send semantics of the running interpreter. Subclasses of the stepping interpreter can define a custom default `stepBlock` and replace the `stepBlock` at runtime.

The debugger itself is implemented by providing different kinds of blocks to the stepping interpreter. The default `stepBlock` of the debugger is implemented as follows:

```
defaultStepBlock
    ↑ [ :receiver :class :message :action |
       self print: receiver class name, '>>', message.
       self debugShellWithAction: action ].
```

It first displays information about the current message send by printing out the receiver's class and the message including the selector and arguments. Then the debug shell is launched, a simple *read-eval-print*-loop (REPL) that accepts certain debug actions, as well as Pinocchio statements as input. Since this REPL runs within the execution context of the interpreter, the current execution of the application is temporarily halted until the REPL eventually returns and decides to evaluate the `action`.

Other types of debug actions can be implemented using different stepping blocks. The following method implements the *step over* behavior. It lets the debugger execute an entire application-level recursive call without prompting the user about its evaluation.

```
stepOver: overAction
    |result previousBlock|
    previousBlock ← stepBlock.
    stepBlock ← [ :receiver :class :message :action |
                    action value ].
    result ← overAction value.
    stepBlock ← previousBlock.
    ↑ result
```

It locally stores the previous stepping strategy and installs a block that skips all steps. Whenever the application finishes the recursive call that triggered the current step the control flow will automatically end up back in this method restoring the block to the previous version and continuing.

Evaluation This way of implementing a debugger is straightforward and only requires very little code to add new flexible features. The whole implementation of the debugger adds around 50 lines of code to the stepping interpreter, which adds another 30 to the vanilla interpreter. Since the debugger is just another interpreter it can be passed in at any level of interpretation. As such it can be used not only to debug a user program, but also the interpreter running it. Naturally this allows for the debugger to debug itself.

6.2.2 Alias Interpreter

As a second use case we show how to implement Object Flow Analysis [92] in Pinocchio. Object Flow Analysis is a dynamic analysis that tracks the transfer of object references at runtime. It has been employed for various reverse engineering approaches and for the implementation of an efficient back-in-time debugger [94].

The problem tackled by Object Flow Analysis is the fact that in code with assignments it is hard to track where a certain value comes from. A debugger only shows the current call stack and hence often does not reveal the context in which a field was assigned. While execution traces show exactly how the interpreter goes through the code, they do not show how the values are stored and retrieved. For example, to understand where a certain value of an instance variable comes from, we need to look at all the source code that might have triggered a store. In an alias interpreter (the back-end used by Object Flow Analysis) object references are represented by real objects on the heap. These objects, referred to as *aliases*, keep track of the origin of each reference in memory.

To know where each value comes from, the alias interpreter alters the semantics of the interactions so that it generates aliases for:

- allocation of objects and their instance variables,
- reading and writing of fields,
- passing of arguments,
- returning of return values, and
- evaluation of literals (constants).

Rather than directly passing around actual values, in the interpreter objects are wrapped into alias objects.

We chose Object Flow Analysis as second use case because it requires deep changes in the interpreter and its object model. This case lets us evaluate how flexible our approach is for extending low-level details of the runtime and how much effort is saved in realizing these changes compared to the original implementation.

An Alias Example Suppose we have a class Person with one instance variable name and simple accessors for name, consider for example the following code:

```
testMethod
    ↑ AliasInterpreter interpret: [ |person|
        person ← Person new.
        person name: 'John'.
        person name: 'Doe'.
        person ].
```

In this excerpt, the block is evaluated in the context of an alias interpreter. All the values used by the alias interpreter are aliased. When the result is returned from the alias interpreter it is not unwrapped so we can inspect the aliasing in the instance. The resulting alias graph, as shown in Figure 6.3, contains the following information:

```
return2 ← self testMethod.

self assert: (return2 isKindOf: ReturnAlias).
self assert: (return2 environment selector = #testMethod).

person ← return2 value.
self assert: (person isKindOf: Person).

return1 ← return2 origin.
self assert: (return1 isKindOf: ReturnAlias).
self assert: (return1 environment selector =  #new).
```

```
fieldWrite2 ← person name.
self assert: (fieldWrite2 isKindOf: FieldWriteAlias).
self assert: (fieldWrite2 value = 'Doe').

fieldWrite1 ← fieldWrite2 predecessor.
self assert: (fieldWrite1 isKindOf: FieldWriteAlias).
self assert: (fieldWrite1 value = 'John').

allocation1 ← fieldWrite1 predecessor.
self assert: (allocation1 isKindOf: AllocationAlias).

parameter1 ← fieldWrite1 origin.
self assert: (parameter1 isKindOf: ParameterAlias).
self assert: (parameter1 value = 'John').

literal1 ← parameter1 origin.
self assert: (literal1 isKindOf: LiteralAlias).
self assert: (literal1 value = 'John').

parameter2 ← fieldWrite2 origin.
self assert: (parameter2 isKindOf: ParameterAlias).
self assert: (parameter2 value = 'Doe').

literal2 ← parameter2 origin.
self assert: (literal2 isKindOf: LiteralAlias).
self assert: (literal2 value = 'Doe').
```

All the gathered information can be used by a debugger to provide means to navigate through the tracked flow of objects. This can easily be used to track for example where null-pointers come from, since all objects are accounted for by aliases.

Linguistic Symbiosis In order to track aliasing the interpreter wraps all objects into alias objects. This makes the object model of the alias interpreter differ significantly from the default interpreter.

Pinocchio's object model provides structural reflection similar to that of Smalltalk. This feature is a requirement for *symbiotic reflection* [150, 68]: applications have to be able to start a new interpreter and pass themselves as applications. The new interpreter starts by running at the base-level of the application, but as the application passes itself to the new interpreter, it becomes part of the meta-level of the application. The new interpreter makes use of base-level structural reflection to interpret the code of the application.

Symbiotic reflection is typically used when the language of the meta-level differs from that of the base-level, for example, when Java is used to interpret a dynamic language. Objects from the meta-level (*e.g.*, Java) typically need to be wrapped before they can be used at the base-level, and unwrapped to be manipulated at the meta-level. This process is known, respectively, as *downing* and *upping*.

6.2. Implementing Custom Interpreters

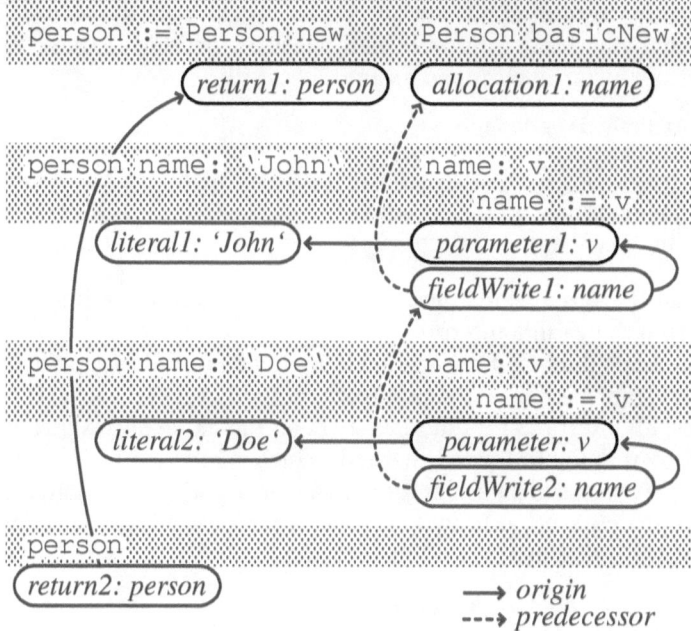

Figure 6.3: Alias Graph (*origin* denotes where an alias comes from, *predecessor* of a field write alias is the alias that was previously stored in this field)

In Pinocchio the base- and the meta-languages generally differ only in limited ways at the meta-level, leaving most of the base-level semantics unaltered. This allows many of the user-defined interpreters to let objects flow freely from the meta-level to the base-level and back, transferring or sharing ownership of the same object without any wrapping or unwrapping. This is the case for the debugger in the previous section.

In case the base- and meta-levels of a Pinocchio interpreter diverge significantly however, it is entirely up to the interpreter to correctly realize the required upping and downing. The alias interpreter is such an example. Rather than directly passing objects from the meta-level to the base-level, all objects passed around in the alias interpreter have to be wrapped into alias objects. When the base-level application performs native actions on aliased objects they first need to be unwrapped by the interpreter. In this situation it is increasingly important that the system relies on *dependency injection* [62, 129] to access static resources, so that wrapped objects are not accidentally leaked to the outside system.

Aliasing using first-class interpreters The implementation of an alias interpreter using Pinocchio is fairly straightforward. First all interpreter methods that are related to one of the tracked actions (object allocation, reading and writing of fields, passing as argument, evaluation of literals (constants) and returning from method) are overridden to generate the aliases. For example, the method that interprets methods is overridden so that it returns a `ReturnAlias` instance wrapped around the result:

```
interpretMethod: aMethod
    | result |
    result ← super interpretMethod: aMethod.
    ↑ (ReturnAlias alias: result)
        environment: environment.
```

Notice that the actual semantics of the interpretation of methods is just inherited from the vanilla interpreter.

All methods that need the actual values inside the aliases are overridden to first unwrap the aliases. Aside from methods related to the evaluation of natives, all interpreter methods only need the value of the current `self`. This is shown in the following method, which is invoked by the interpreter whenever it evaluates an assignment to a slot. It assigns the actual value to the slot of the current `self` by first unwrapping the aliased `self` and then wrapping the value in a `FieldWriteAlias`:

```
assignSlot: aSlot to: anAlias
    | alias unwrappedSelf |
    unwrappedSelf ← self currentSelf value.
    alias ← (FieldWriteAlias alias: anAlias)
            environment: environment.
    alias predecessor: (aSlot readFrom: unwrappedSelf).
    ↑ aSlot assign: alias on: unwrappedSelf
```

The alias interpreter uses a different object model for the base-level than for the meta-level. As explained in the previous paragraph this requires the alias interpreter to realize the upping and downing by itself. Every time an object moves from the meta-level to the base-level it needs to be wrapped to look like the other objects in the runtime (like aliases, in this case).

There are two places where objects potentially flow from the meta-level to the base-level. The first is the initial closure passed to the interpreter. The closure is linked to an environment that contains objects possibly referred to by the code of the closure. Rather than directly sending value to the closure, we first have to pre-process it:

```
interpret: aClosure
    ↑ self send: (Message new selector: #value)
        to: aClosure asAliased
```

The `asAliased` message will deep-clone the closure, and wrap the closure as well as all the values referred to by its environment into allocation aliases. We use allocation aliases since we are unsure of the origin of the objects. As it is the initial state of the alias interpreter, from the perspective of the alias interpreter it is as if the objects were allocated at that point in time. This indicates that users of interpreters that rely on a modified object model have to be careful not to pass a closure along that has references to huge object graphs or ensure that deep-cloning is not required by the interpreter.

The second place where objects flow from the base-level to the meta-level and back is in the evaluation of natives. To support the interpretation of natives, the original alias interpreter overrides most of the supported methods and performs the correct action. Since not all natives have the same semantics, no single implementation can properly support the evaluation of all of them. To complete our implementation we would also have to provide new implementations for the subset of operations we support. For this experiment, however, we limited ourselves to the general solution that works for most examples. Whenever a native is called, the receiver as well as the arguments are downed and passed to the implementation of the meta-interpreter. The result returned from this native is upped by wrapping it into an allocation alias and passed to the application.

Evaluation The original Object Flow Analysis has been implemented by directly extending the Pharo VM. It required changes of a large amount of the VM code and took several weeks to implement. The Pinocchio version on the other hand was implemented in less than one day. It is spread over 20 methods and 12 alias data classes.

One of the main ideas behind the alias interpreter is that it allocates aliases on the heap so they are automatically garbage collected when their state becomes irrelevant to the state of the application. Because the extension is at the VM level new objects have to be manually instantiated at that level. Since referring to specific Smalltalk classes is cumbersome from within the interpreter, the original interpreter just provides one class fitting all types of aliases. This class has a special field designated to indicate the actual alias type. In Pinocchio, the alias interpreter is implemented in a standard Smalltalk environment. This allows the programmer to rely on the full expressiveness of the language: all aliases are instances of classes representing their specific type. Since Pinocchio interpreters reuse garbage collection from the main runtime, it is also automatically used for collecting the aliases.

In contrast to the original alias debugger the Pinocchio version is fully hosted within the language itself. This allows us to use the standard tools for implementing, and more importantly, for debugging the alias interpreter. Now that the alias interpreter is functional new tools or even alias interpreters can be debugged using the current alias interpreter. This is not possible in the original Smalltalk version, since their alias interpreter extensions are written in C, and are thus not subject to the (modified) Smalltalk interpreter.

6.2.3 Recursive Interpreters

Behavioral reflection in Smalltalk entails manipulation of the (reified) runtime stack. In Smalltalk-80, the state of the computation is fully captured by the runtime stack. As a consequence, the Smalltalk bytecode interpreter does not need to keep track of any control flow itself and automatically adapts to reflective changes to the runtime stack. The disadvantage of this approach is that to be able to adapt to such reflective changes easily, the evaluation of the interpreter is completely decoupled from the evaluation of the application. Not only must bytecodes explicitly manipulate the stack, but code that passes control from the meta-level to the base-level must be "ripped" into event handlers that can run to completion without blocking [2]. Since base-level code in Smalltalk-80 can make arbitrary changes to the runtime stack, the bytecode interpreter must be prepared to resume execution in any arbitrary context. If the interpreter wants to keep track of state related to the evaluation of the application other than what is available in the standard stack frames, it also has to manually keep track of this data and keep it in sync with the application's execution.

Pinocchio's use of first-class interpreters with *automatic stack management* [2] greatly simplifies the expression of behavioral reflection. Code that passes control from the meta-level to the base-level can be straightforwardly implemented by relying on recursive calls. Pinocchio interpreters can simply rely on recursion to keep track of any state related to the application's control flow just like any other Smalltalk application.

The disadvantage of this approach is that it becomes impossible to directly perform operations normally requiring explicit stack manipulations since there is no explicit stack. We identify two types of direct stack manipulation in Smalltalk: applications need to be able to (i) capture a certain state of the stack and later restore it, and (ii) capture a stack and pass it to another program, a meta-circular interpreter, for reflective evaluation of the application. In this section we show that Pinocchio supports these two requirements respectively through first-class continuations [34] and modifiable first-class interpreters.

Parallel Debugging An example of a situation where a user would like to capture and restore the state of a stack is a *parallel debugger*. Unlike the normal debugger, which only evaluates one block at a time, this special kind of debugger takes two blocks and interprets them in parallel comparing their state of evaluation at each step.

Consider the following failing test case, which we encountered during the development of Pinocchio:

```
dict ← SetBucket new.
dict at: #key put: 'value'.

self assert: (dict includes: #key).
self assert: (dict includes: 'key').
```

The second assertion (last line) fails. This test was documenting a bug that we had difficulties to track down. Symbols and strings are considered equal (#key = 'key') in Smalltalk and hence the second assertion should pass too.

Using the basic debugger described in subsection 6.2.1 to find the difference in execution of the two assertions is cumbersome. The manual approach would be to launch a separate debugger for each of the assertions and step through the code until the states of the tests differ.

Since we had difficulties tracking down the root cause of this bug, we implemented a specialized debugger that we call *parallel debugger*. The use of the parallel debugger for the previously mentioned test case looks as follows:

```
ParallelDebugger interpret:
    (Array
        with: [ dict includes: #key ]
        with: [ dict includes: 'key' ])
```

The debugger runs the given blocks in parallel up to the point where the executions start to differ:

```
SetBucket>>#includes:
    SetBucket>>#do:
        SmallInt(1)>>#to:do:
            BlockClosure>>#whileTrue:
                SmallInt(1)>>#<=
                    SmallInt(1)>>#>
                        ⟶    false
                    false>>#not
                        ⟶    true
                true>>#ifTrue:
                    SetBucket>>#at:
                        ⟶    #'key'
                    Symbol(#'key')>>#==
                    1) (#'key')    ⟶    true
                    2) ('key')     ⟶    false
```

Listing 6.1: Parallel debugger trace

Looking at this trace immediately reveals that both traces differ upon a strict equality check on a symbol. In the first case the comparison returns `true`, in the second case `false`. SetBucket incorrectly uses `==` (pointer equality) rather than `=` to compare keys, rendering strings and symbols distinct. The parallel debugger provides the minimal output needed to quickly identify the root cause of the problem.

To implement the parallel debugger we need to be able to evaluate multiple closures in lock step. In an interpreter with manual stack management this is straightforward. Rather than interpreting the code of one interpreter in a loop, one lets all interpreters do one step of evaluation before comparing their states. Pinocchio however relies on automatic stack management and thus relies on recursion to evaluate the closures. This implies that the

99

Chapter 6. First-Class Interpreters

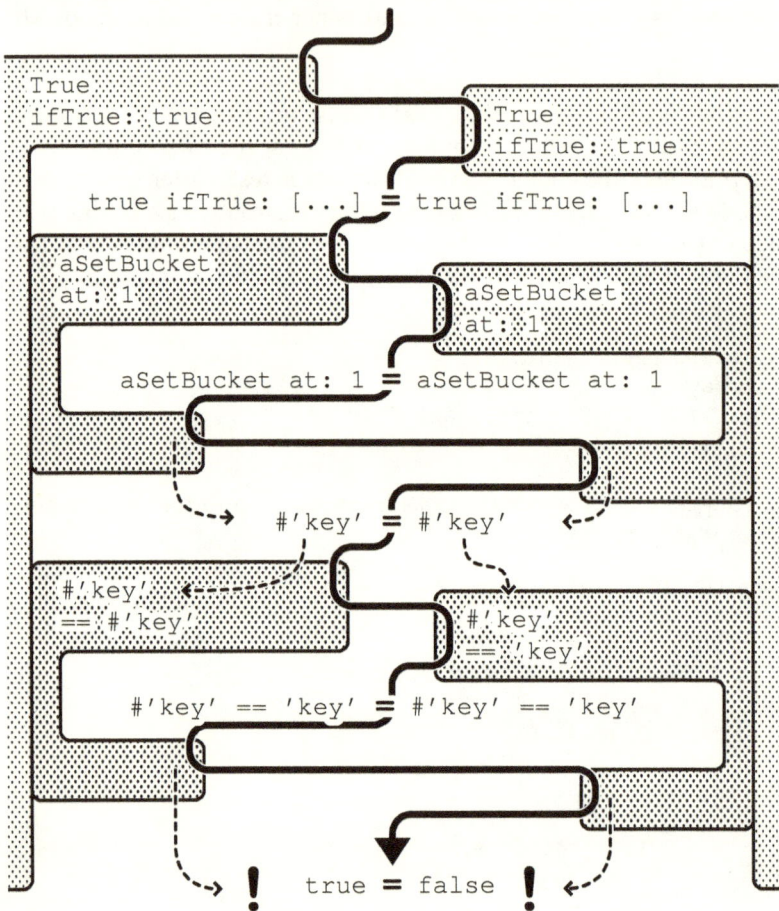

Figure 6.4: Thread-based parallel execution of two code parts in the parallel debugger.

parallel debugger needs to be able to jump out of, and back into a certain recursion state. This problem is similar to implementing coroutines in a recursive language. The only difference is that the parallel debugger itself handles thread-switching before and after each message send. Coroutines and threads can easily be accommodated in recursive languages through the use of first-class continuations [71].

Just like the debugger described in subsection 6.2.1, the parallel debugger is built as a subclass of the stepping interpreter. The main difference is that the stepping block is not used to control a single execution trace, but to handle the interleaved execution of the given number of closures. Before and after each message send, control is transferred to the next thread: The

100

state of the current green thread[2] is stored by capturing its continuation and the application's environment. The next green thread is then continued by restoring its application's environment, and by activating its continuation. Whenever we resume the first thread, we compare the state of all the routines and continue with the first thread.

The parallel debugger, like the serial debugger presented in Section 6.1, directly reuses the object model of the underlying base-level interpreter. As a consequence, no upping or downing is required, and objects can freely flow between the base- and meta-levels.

Even though interpreters are defined recursively as AST visitors, this poses no problem for expressing non-local flow of control. Green threads are easily simulated by capturing the needed continuations and explicitly transferring control when needed (in the case of parallel debuggers, before and after each message send). The parallel debugger is only possible due to the support for continuations in Pinocchio. Without continuations we could not switch between the execution of multiple closures. It would only be possible to continue the execution of the next closure from inside the current one.

Runtime Modifiable Interpreters Meta-circular interpreters such as the Smalltalk debugger are a second type of application that require direct access to an explicit stack. The Smalltalk interpreter can pass control over the evaluation of an application to a debugger by passing its runtime stack to the debugger. The Smalltalk debugger however is fully meta-circular and has to manually manage this runtime stack for the evaluation of the application. The advantage of this approach is that since the meta-circular as well as the core interpreter are both decoupled from the state of the application's stack, the meta-circular interpreter is given full control over the evaluation of the application. While Pinocchio's first-class interpreters only have continuous behavioral impact on the evaluation until the closure finishes, meta-circular interpreters with manual stack management can evaluate the program beyond the continuation where the interpreter was started. This is a very useful feature as is obvious from the Smalltalk debugger. Whenever an error occurs, the Smalltalk debugger can take over the evaluation as if it had been running the application all along, although the core interpreter has mostly executed the program up to that point.

If in Pinocchio we would like to start a new interpreter to change the interpretation semantics, the change would be limited to the scope of the control flow in which they were activated. This is undesirable for debugging purposes since we would not be able to step through more of the program than the recursion of the message send that caused the error. We rather want to change the semantics of an interpreter while it is running.

In Pinocchio modifiable interpreters are accommodated by letting the

---

[2]The parallel debugger manages green threads, since it emulates true multi-threading by alternating between the different green threads on a single hardware thread.

user specify which parts of an interpreter are mutable. The stepping interpreter discussed in subsection 6.2.1 is an example of an interpreter whose semantics can partly be modified while it is running. Its `stepBlock` influencing the semantics of message sends is orthogonal to the control flow of the application, leaving it unaffected by the interpreter exiting the control flow where the `stepBlock` was installed. The semantics of the `stepBlock` is only bound to the scope in which its host interpreter is active.

The following example is an extension method to the debugger described in subsection 6.2.1. It temporarily replaces the current stepping semantics for the duration of a variable number of message sends. It allows a user to specify a specific number of steps to be skipped.

```
skipBlock: count
    |skips previousBlock|
    skips ← 0.
    previousBlock ← self stepBlock.
    ↑ [ :receiver :class :message :action |
        skips ← skips + 1.
        (skips >= count)
            ifTrue: [ self stepBlock: previousBlock ].
        self executeAction: action ].
```

For the duration of the given number of message sends the user is not prompted concerning the evaluation. Once the steps are over, control is returned to the previously active stepping style.

The `skipBlock:` method is a clear example of how the `stepBlock` can be used to apply changes that potentially surpass the control flow in which they were activated. Even if the number of skipped steps is larger than the number of steps needed for the application-level recursive call before which the block was installed, the block will stay active until the requested number of steps are over.

6.3 Minimizing the Interpreter Stack

Our approach of starting new interpreters on top of other interpreters is similar to, albeit the inverse of, the tower of first-class interpreters in Refci [133]. This has the advantage that we can use the same approach to minimize the height of the tower that is actually running at each point in time. For example, since normal applications are not interpreted, the stack of interpreters is empty. It is important to never run on a stack bigger than necessary, since each extra level of interpretation has a steep price in terms of performance.

Since most custom interpreters will only partly alter the semantics of existing native methods, the default implementation in charge of invoking natives, `invokeNative`, allows interpreters to rely on meta-meta-level implementations of natives to provide the behavior to the base-level. In other words, whenever an application ends up in code that invokes a native, the interpreter can ask its meta-interpreter to perform the actual invocation of the native. This temporarily drops the interpreter from the active stack of interpreters.

In Pinocchio the height of the tower is further pragmatically minimized by using invokeNative. By making the whole standard interpreter available as a fine-grained set of natives installed on the Interpreter class (see Figure 6.1), only the extensions to the interpreter are evaluated meta-circularly. The reused native methods are evaluated directly at the bottom level.

Since natives are able to send messages back to the application level, every call to invokeNative stores the interpreter that triggered the actual native. To ensure that the application always runs on the proper level of interpretation, when the native wants to send a message back to the application it first has to restore the stack of interpreters that was active before invoking the native. An example of such a case is the native implementation of the at: method installed on dictionaries. This method needs to be able to request the hash value of a key, and later compare it with the keys in the dictionary using the = message. Both methods are within the control flow of the native evaluation of the at: method. To evaluate both methods at the right level of interpretation, the stack of interpreters that was active before the at: was invoked needs to be reconstructed before their evaluation is started.

6.4 Performance

We indicate the expected performance ceiling by running a simple benchmark, calculating the 27th Fibonacci number, on a fully meta-circular implementation of the interpreter. We benchmark the interpreter running on top of Pinocchio implemented as simple bytecode interpreter, as well as the bytecode interpreter itself. On an average of 10 consecutive runs, the native interpreter executes the code in an average time of 0.09 seconds, whereas the meta-circular interpreter takes 25.60 seconds. The meta-circular interpreter thus executes 250 times slower than the native interpreter. This is the expected cost for each extra level of interpretation without optimizations.

The benchmarked version of Pinocchio calculates the 35th Fibonacci number in 2.5 seconds, and is thus more than 10 times slower than the version described in Chapter 4. We expect that, for a single additional level of interpretation, a faster runtime will make the first-class interpreter approach more feasible.

For further research, it is also interesting to look into dynamic optimization techniques that can bring the performance of applications running on top of custom interpreters close to the speed of standard applications. This essentially removes one meta-level. Previous research [17, 151] has outlined how meta-level tracing can optimize code that is running on top of an interpreter, without needing to implement a compiler that knows about the semantics of the interpreter. The idea is to run the application on top of an interpreter, that is in turn running in a JIT compiling environment. Straightforward tracing of the interpreter would over time, however, compile the single bytecode implementations as separate native functions. This brings its performance maximally to that of a simple interpreter written in native code. However, by also passing the program counter of the application in the interpreter to the tracing facility, the JIT compiler can trace how the interpreter evaluates the application. This approach allows the compiler to implicitly compile the application by tracing the application through the interpreter. The dynamic compiler, in essence, expands the base-level expressions using the meta-level interpreter code that evaluates it, optimizes the expanded code, and executes the result as native meta-level code. In the ideal scenario, this would completely remove superfluous interpretation overhead for a single layer of interpretation.

6.5 Related Work

In this section we compare our approach to the reflective interpreters techniques, as well as meta-circular interpreters.

6.5.1 Tower Approach to First-Class Interpreters

Of all reflective interpreters, our model is most similar to the model proposed by Simmons *et al.* in their prototype Refci [133]. Just like Pinocchio, Refci provides access to first-class extensible interpreters. Their preliminary procedures are the equivalent of having functions that create anonymous subclasses of a existing interpreter classes, overriding single interpreter methods (or implementing a single new interpreter methods).

Unlike Refci interpreters, Pinocchio's interpreters are not tail-recursive continuation passing interpreters (by default). Instead they are normal recursive interpreters that rely on the continuation of the runtime below to maintain their continuation. This greatly simplifies the final definition of the actual interpreter since control flow is handled implicitly. It however does not restrict the power of the interpreter since continuations can be captured and restored. In Refci such an implementation would be impractical since tail-recursion is used to ensure that the theoretically infinite tower of interpreters can be cut off to a finite stack of actually running interpreters and an unbounded meta-continuation of waiting interpreters.

Refci provides no model to share extensions between different interpreters in the stack. Duplicate changes need to be installed manually in the levels where they are required. In Pinocchio subclassing takes care of the sharing of code. Since in Pinocchio interpreters are manually stacked, these interpreters can be instances of the same interpreter thus automatically sharing extensions.

We go beyond the Refci model, by showing (in Section 6.2.3) how Pinocchio interpreters can be made modifiable at run time. The first-class interpreters themselves can decide what is made modifiable. The modifications applied to an interpreter in Pinocchio can have further extent than the recursion in which they were created. In Refci this notion of extended continuations was merely noted as future work.

No effort was made to outline how Refci can be made into a practical runtime. Since all interpreters in Refci are meta-circular, it thus suffers from the problems explained in subsection 6.5.2.

6.5.2 Meta-circular Interpreters

Meta-circular interpreters [1] such as the Smalltalk debugger and all uncompiled versions of the interpreters described in Section 3.2 offer a way of easily allowing changes to the semantics of a language at runtime from within the language itself. They generally reify a subset of features from the host-language, and reuse the complementary set of features.

The first problem with meta-circular interpreters is that to modify their semantics one generally needs to directly modify the source code. No extension mechanisms are provided by the interpreters themselves. Pinocchio on the other hand provides a clear protocol for extension through subclassing.

The second problem is that meta-circular interpreters impose a large runtime overhead in comparison with standard interpreters. This problem is partly solved by compilation of the full interpreter, as discussed in Section 3.2, but this results in a compile-time rather than run-time change, resulting in immutable interpretation semantics at run time.

While in the current implementation of Pinocchio the `Interpreter` class is still mostly meta-circular, a clear strategy of how performance can be greatly increased has been outlined. We explained how to rely as much as possible on the existing C-level interpreter, essentially removing the meta-circular layer for all code except for the custom interpreter extensions. Then we explained how these extensions to the interpreter can also be optimized at runtime through JIT compilation.

6.5.3 Dealing with Infinity

Brown [148] is an extension of 3-Lisp that introduced the *meta-continuation* as an explicit representation of the infinite tower of interpreters. As shown in Figure 6.5, the theoretically infinite tower of interpreters can be implemented as a finite stack of interpreters running on top of a *level-shifting processor* — a non-reflective processor that is able to *shift up* a level whenever a reification occurs in the application, *i.e.*, go up one meta-level. In order to stay efficient the processor is also able to *shift down* whenever a level of interpretation is not needed anymore. An application should ultimately never run at a level higher than is necessary. Shifting up is implemented in Brown by popping an interpreter from the meta-continuation, a lazy infinite stack of interpreters. Shifting down pushes the unneeded interpreter back onto the meta-continuation.

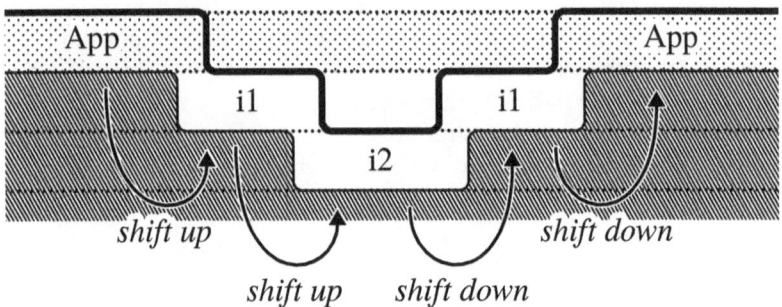

Figure 6.5: Finite Scope of the Infinite Tower of Interpreters

As explained in Section 6.3, Pinocchio uses this technique to minimize its finite stack of interpreters.

6.6 Summary

First-class interpreters inherit their object model from Smalltalk, except for the fact that "compiled" methods are reified as ASTs rather than directly as the code format used by the native execution engine. While running an application on top of a custom interpreter, objects can freely flow between base- and meta-levels provided their structural representation remains the same. Otherwise the customized interpreter is responsible for upping and downing objects between levels. Interpreters are defined recursively, but have a fine degree of control over program flow due to their ability to capture and transfer control to first-class continuations. Garbage collection, and other native features provided by the native meta-level can be simply reused by specialized interpreters.

We have shown through several examples how behavioral reflection provided by first-class interpreters allows sophisticated behavioral adaptations to be easily implemented. In addition to a serial and a parallel debugger, we demonstrated how an alias interpreter, which tracks object flow for back-in-time debugging, can be easily implemented by a specialized interpreter, in contrast to a conventional approach in Smalltalk requiring invasive changes to create a specialized VM.

The first-class interpreters are presently a proof-of-concept prototype implemented on top of an older version of Pinocchio. No serious optimization effort has yet been undertaken. We have outlined a number of promising tracks that we believe will significantly reduce the overhead introduced by specializing an interpreter, including simply porting the model to the latest version of Pinocchio.

7
Conclusions

In this dissertation we have identified *communication between objects, semantics of object state*, and *interpretation of code* as three building blocks fundamental to object-oriented runtimes. We showed that by reifying them into the runtime we open up the language. We provided full implementations with realistic performance for all the contributions.

Our key contributions are the following:

- By implementing a generic message passing protocol we have limited the assumptions objects impose on their communication partners. Through the unification of meta- and base-level code we have attained polymorphism at the meta-level, supporting fine-grained customization through a behavioral MOP. We showed that using this building block we can 1) customize the meta-level with base-level objects, and 2) modify the semantics of message lookup. (Chapter 4)

- By introducing first-class structural metaobjects we have bridged the gap between high-level object features and the low-level physical layout. We showed that using these building blocks we can 1) provide behavioral hooks to object layouts that are triggered when the fields of an object are accessed, 2) compose multiple slots into a custom low-level representation and 3) simplify the implementation of state-related language extensions such as stateful traits. (Chapter 5)

- We have extended the behavioral reflective model of Pinocchio with first-class AST interpreters, separated from the low-level language implementation. We have showed that first-class interpreters easily support non-trivial debuggers. (Chapter 6)

7.1 Future Work

In this section we provide an overview of further research and practical next steps related to the implementation of Pinocchio.

7.1.1 Research Directions

Structural dependencies. By establishing a calling convention, in Chapter 4 we limited the dependency on the expected encoding of behavior. While this provides greater flexibility for executed code, it means that every message send is essentially a foreign function call. This implies that we need to design a memory management system that can cope with diverse languages, especially manually managed languages, and the flow of data between them. This may mean that the presented conventions need make the management of passed data explicit.

Negotiating object features. In Chapter 5, we have shown that the layout model supports slots that require special structural features, using layout scopes (*e.g.*, `BitSlot` requires a free bit in a `BitFieldScope`, see subsection 5.3.1). A problem with the current implementation is that a pragmatic approach was taken to support such slots. The slots directly extend the inherited layout scopes to include missing layout scopes. This, however, allows slots to mutate the chain of inherited layout scopes, or discard it altogether. Instances of the resulting class will be inconsistent with the inherited code that operates on them, likely ending in invalid memory access. Instead, slots should use a well-designed communication API to require object features. The API should ensure that slots can only add new features. This may imply replacing layout scopes by another model that better captures structural object features.

Describing arrays. Currently layouts only apply to regular Smalltalk objects. It would be interesting to investigate how the model would also apply for the arrayed portion of arrayed objects. For example, by attaching a type to the array we can imagine supporting inlined objects that have better cache locality than arrays containing objects via references. This would be beneficial for the standard Pharo dictionary implementation that normally contains `Association` instances, objects that contain a key-value pair. Rather than linking to the `Association` instance, the key-value could directly be inlined in two consecutive entries, without the user of the array having to be aware of this fact.

By extending the feature-set related to the state of arrays, the resulting language moves in the direction of object-oriented databases.

Context state as a building block. The list of identified building blocks is not exhaustive. One additional block we already identify is the state of the current execution context. By reifying state manipulation within a context frame (reading from and assigning to local variables) we essentially support active variables [60, 5], local variables that behave just like our slots, which are read from and written to using access methods rather than directly using primitive operations. This feature is useful for example to implement contextual values [139]. Given that activations in Self are clones of the method, the layout model might be reusable in that setting to directly support active values without the need to extend the model.

7.1.2 Practical Steps

Reintegrating results. The different approaches presented in this dissertation have mostly been developed in isolation. Given that the runtime explained in Chapter 4 is the latest version, both first-class layouts and first-class debuggers should be reintegrated into that version.

Polishing Pinocchio. To evolve Pinocchio into a robust Smalltalk runtime, the compiler needs to be finished; memory management and multithreading need to be implemented; and a multitude of primitives needs to be supported.

Static single assignment. The Pinocchio implementation went through several stages of rewrites to improve performance while getting closer to the hardware. Since during development it was used as a platform for learning how to generate self-supporting native code, the compiler based on three address code (TAC) is reaching its limitations and is currently holding up development. To increase progress, effort needs to be put into replacing the TAC compiler by a compiler based on static single assignment form. This effort would also pay off for implementing further optimizations, enabling both static and dynamic optimizations through peephole optimizations and inlining.

Chapter 7. Conclusions

Bibliography

[1] Harold Abelson, Gerald Jay Sussman, and Julie Sussman. *Structure and interpretation of computer programs*. MIT electrical engineering and computer science series. McGraw-Hill, 1991. Available from: http://mitpress.mit.edu/sicp/full-text/book/book.html.

[2] Atul Adya, Jon Howell, Marvin Theimer, William J. Bolosky, and John R. Douceur. Cooperative task management without manual stack management. In *ATEC '02: Proceedings of the General Track of the annual conference on USENIX Annual Technical Conference*, pages 289–302, Berkeley, CA, USA, 2002. USENIX Association.

[3] Ole Agesen and Urs Hölzle. Type feedback vs. concrete type inference: A comparison of optimization techniques for object-oriented languages. In *Proceedings of the Tenth Annual Conference on Object-Oriented Programming Systems, Languages, and Applications*, OOPSLA '95, pages 91–107, New York, NY, USA, 1995. ACM. doi:10.1145/217838.217847.

[4] Gerald Aigner and Urs Hölzle. Eliminating virtual function calls in C++ programs. In P. Cointe, editor, *Proceedings ECOOP '96*, volume 1098 of *LNCS*, pages 142–166, Linz, Austria, July 1996. Springer-Verlag.

[5] Thomas H. Austin, Tim Disney, and Cormac Flanagan. Virtual values for language extension. *SIGPLAN Not.*, 46:921–938, October 2011. doi:10.1145/2076021.2048136.

[6] Lars Bak, Gilad Bracha, Steffen Grarup, Robert Griesemer, David Griswold, and Urs Hölzle. Mixins in Strongtalk. In *ECOOP '02 Workshop on Inheritance*, June 2002.

[7] Roland Barcia, Geoffrey Hambrick, Kyle Brown, Robert Peterson, and Kulvir Bhogal. *Persistence in the enterprise: a guide to persistence technologies*. IBM Press, first edition, 2008.

[8] Kent Beck and Erich Gamma. Test infected: Programmers love writing tests. *Java Report*, 3(7):51–56, 1998. Available from: http://members.pingnet.ch/gamma/junit.htm.

[9] James R. Bell. Threaded code. *Commun. ACM*, 16:370–372, June 1973. doi:10.1145/362248.362270.

[10] Alexandre Bergel, Stéphane Ducasse, Oscar Nierstrasz, and Roel Wuyts. Stateful traits and their formalization. *Journal of Computer Languages, Systems and Structures*, 34(2-3):83–108, 2008. Available from: http://scg.unibe.ch/archive/papers/Berg08eStatefulTraits.pdf, doi:10.1016/j.cl.2007.05.003.

[11] Alexandre Bergel, Stéphane Ducasse, and Lukas Renggli. Seaside – advanced composition and control flow for dynamic web applications. *ERCIM News*, 72, January 2008. Available from: http://ercim-news.ercim.org/content/view/325/536/.

[12] Emery D. Berger, Kathryn S. McKinley, Robert D. Blumofe, and Paul R. Wilson. Hoard: a scalable memory allocator for multi-threaded applications. *SIGPLAN Not.*, 35:117–128, November 2000. doi:10.1145/356989.357000.

[13] M. Berndl, B. Vitale, M. Zaleski, and A.D. Brown. Context threading: a flexible and efficient dispatch technique for virtual machine interpreters. In *Code Generation and Optimization, 2005. CGO 2005. International Symposium on*, pages 15 – 26, March 2005. doi:10.1109/CGO.2005.14.

[14] Gavin Bierman. First-class relationships in an object-oriented language. In *ECOOP*, pages 262–286. Springer-Verlag, 2005. doi:10.1007/11531142_12.

[15] Andrew Black, Stéphane Ducasse, Oscar Nierstrasz, Damien Pollet, Damien Cassou, and Marcus Denker. *Pharo by Example*. Square Bracket Associates, 2009. Available from: http://pharobyexample.org.

[16] Daniel G. Bobrow, Ken Kahn, Gregor Kiczales, Larry Masinter, Mark Stefik, and Frank Zdybel. Commonloops: Merging lisp and object-oriented programming. In *Proceedings OOPSLA '86, ACM SIGPLAN Notices*, volume 21, pages 17–29, November 1986.

[17] Carl Friedrich Bolz, Antonio Cuni, Maciej Fijalkowski, and Armin Rigo. Tracing the meta-level: Pypy's tracing JIT compiler. In *ICOOOLPS '09: Proceedings of the 4th workshop on the Implementation, Compilation, Optimization of Object-Oriented Languages and Programming Systems*, pages 18–25, New York, NY, USA, 2009. ACM. doi:10.1145/1565824.1565827.

[18] Carl Friedrich Bolz, Adrian Kuhn, Adrian Lienhard, Nicholas D. Matsakis, Oscar Nierstrasz, Lukas Renggli, Armin Rigo, and Toon Verwaest. Back to the future in one week — implementing a

Smalltalk VM in PyPy. In *Self-Sustaining Systems*, volume 5142 of *LNCS*, pages 123–139. Springer, 2008. Available from: http://scg.unibe.ch/archive/papers/Bolz08aSpy.pdf, doi:10.1007/978-3-540-89275-5_7.

[19] Carl Friedrich Bolz and Armin Rigo. How to not write virtual machines for dynamic languages. In *3rd Workshop on Dynamic Languages and Applications*, 2007. Available from: http://dyla2007.unibe.ch/?download=dyla07-HowToNotWriteVMs.pdf.

[20] Chandrasekhar Boyapati, Barbara Liskov, and Liuba Shrira. Ownership types for object encapsulation. In *Principles of Programming Languages (POPL'03)*, pages 213–223. ACM Press, 2003. doi:10.1145/604131.604156.

[21] Gilad Bracha. Executable grammars in Newspeak. *Electron. Notes Theor. Comput. Sci.*, 193:3–18, 2007. Available from: http://bracha.org/executableGrammars.pdf, doi:10.1016/j.entcs.2007.10.004.

[22] Gilad Bracha and William Cook. Mixin-based inheritance. In *Proceedings OOPSLA/ECOOP '90, ACM SIGPLAN Notices*, volume 25, pages 303–311, October 1990.

[23] Gilad Bracha and David Ungar. Mirrors: design principles for meta-level facilities of object-oriented programming languages. In *Proceedings of the International Conference on Object-Oriented Programming, Systems, Languages, and Applications (OOPSLA'04), ACM SIGPLAN Notices*, pages 331–344, New York, NY, USA, 2004. ACM Press. Available from: http://bracha.org/mirrors.pdf, doi:10.1145/1028976.1029004.

[24] John Brant, Brian Foote, Ralph Johnson, and Don Roberts. Wrappers to the rescue. In *Proceedings European Conference on Object Oriented Programming (ECOOP'98)*, volume 1445 of *LNCS*, pages 396–417. Springer-Verlag, 1998.

[25] Randal E. Bryant and David R. O'Hallaron. *Computer Systems: A Programmer's Perspective*. Addison-Wesley Publishing Company, USA, 2nd edition, 2010.

[26] Douglas C. Burger, James R. Goodman, and Alain Kägi. The declining effectiveness of dynamic caching for general-purpose microprocessors. Technical report, University of Wisconsin – Madison. Computer Sciences Dept, 1995.

[27] Brad Calder and Dirk Grunwald. Reducing indirect function call overhead in C++ programs. In *Proceedings of the 21st ACM SIGPLAN-SIGACT symposium on Principles of programming languages*, POPL '94,

pages 397–408, New York, NY, USA, 1994. ACM. doi:10.1145/174675.177973.

[28] David Callahan, Steve Carr, and Ken Kennedy. Improving register allocation for subscripted variables. *SIGPLAN Not.*, 25:53–65, June 1990. doi:10.1145/93548.93553.

[29] Craig Chambers and David Ungar. Customization: optimizing compiler technology for self, a dynamically-typed object-oriented programming language. In *Proceedings of the ACM SIGPLAN 1989 Conference on Programming language design and implementation*, PLDI '89, pages 146–160, New York, NY, USA, 1989. ACM. doi:10.1145/73141.74831.

[30] Craig Chambers, David Ungar, and Elgin Lee. An efficient implementation of SELF — a dynamically-typed object-oriented language based on prototypes. In *Proceedings OOPSLA '89, ACM SIGPLAN Notices*, volume 24, pages 49–70, October 1989.

[31] Haibo Chen, Jie Yu, Rong Chen, Binyu Zang, and Pen-Chung Yew. Polus: A powerful live updating system. In *ICSE '07: Proceedings of the 29th international conference on Software Engineering*, pages 271–281, Washington, DC, USA, 2007. IEEE Computer Society. doi:10.1109/ICSE.2007.65.

[32] Shigeru Chiba, Gregor Kiczales, and John Lamping. Avoiding confusion in metacircularity: The meta-helix. In Kokichi Futatsugi and Satoshi Matsuoka, editors, *Proceedings of ISOTAS '96*, volume 1049 of *Lecture Notes in Computer Science*, pages 157–172. Springer, 1996. Available from: http://www2.parc.com/csl/groups/sda/publications/papers/Chiba-ISOTAS96/for-web.pdf, doi:10.1007/3-540-60954-7_49.

[33] Trishul M. Chilimbi and James R. Larus. Using generational garbage collection to implement cache-conscious data placement. *SIGPLAN Not.*, 34:37–48, October 1998. doi:10.1145/301589.286865.

[34] Christopher T. Haynes Daniel P. Friedman and Eugene Kohlbecker. Programming with continuations. Technical Report 151, Indiana University, November 1984.

[35] Jeffrey Dean, David Grove, and Craig Chambers. Optimization of object-oriented programs using static class hierarchy analysis. In W. Olthoff, editor, *Proceedings ECOOP '95*, volume 952 of *LNCS*, pages 77–101, Aarhus, Denmark, August 1995. Springer-Verlag.

[36] Marcus Denker. *Sub-method Structural and Behavioral Reflection*. PhD thesis, University of Bern, May 2008. Available from: http://scg.unibe.ch/archive/phd/denker-phd.pdf.

[37] Marcus Denker, Stéphane Ducasse, Adrian Lienhard, and Philippe Marschall. Sub-method reflection. In *Journal of Object Technology, Special Issue. Proceedings of TOOLS Europe 2007*, volume 6/9, pages 231–251. ETH, October 2007. Available from: http://www.jot.fm/contents/issue_2007_10/paper14.html, doi:10.5381/jot.2007.6.9.a14.

[38] Marcus Denker, Mathieu Suen, and Stéphane Ducasse. The meta in meta-object architectures. In *Proceedings of TOOLS EUROPE 2008*, volume 11 of *LNBIP*, pages 218–237. Springer-Verlag, 2008. Available from: http://scg.unibe.ch/archive/papers/Denk08bMetaContextLNBIP.pdf, doi:10.1007/978-3-540-69824-1_13.

[39] Jim des Rivières and Brian Cantwell Smith. The implementation of procedurally reflective languages. In *LFP '84: Proceedings of the 1984 ACM Symposium on LISP and functional programming*, pages 331–347, New York, NY, USA, 1984. ACM. doi:10.1145/800055.802050.

[40] David Detlefs and Ole Agesen. Inlining of virtual methods. In R. Guerraoui, editor, *Proceedings ECOOP '99*, volume 1628 of *LNCS*, pages 258–278, Lisbon, Portugal, June 1999. Springer-Verlag.

[41] L. Peter Deutsch and Allan M. Schiffman. Efficient implementation of the Smalltalk-80 system. In *Proceedings POPL '84*, Salt Lake City, Utah, January 1984. Available from: http://webpages.charter.net/allanms/popl84.pdf, doi:10.1145/800017.800542.

[42] Theo D'Hondt. Are bytecodes an atavism? In *Self-Sustaining Systems: First Workshop, S3 2008 Potsdam, Germany, May 15-16, 2008 Revised Selected Papers*, pages 140–155. Springer-Verlag, Berlin, Heidelberg, 2008. doi:10.1007/978-3-540-89275-5_8.

[43] Django. http://www.djangoproject.com.

[44] Rémi Douence and Mario Südholt. A generic reification technique for object-oriented reflective languages. *Higher Order Symbol. Comput.*, 14(1):7–34, 2001. doi:10.1023/A:1011549115358.

[45] Ulrich Drepper. What every programmer should know about memory. Technical report, Red Hat, Inc., November 2007. Available from: http://www.akkadia.org/drepper/cpumemory.pdf.

[46] Karel Driesen and Urs Hölzle. The direct cost of virtual function calls in C++. In *Proceedings of the 11th ACM SIGPLAN conference on Object-oriented programming, systems, languages, and applications*, OOPSLA '96, pages 306–323, New York, NY, USA, 1996. ACM. doi:10.1145/236337.236369.

[47] Karel Driesen, Urs Hölzle, and Jan Vitek. Message dispatch on pipelined processors. In W. Olthoff, editor, *Proceedings ECOOP '95*, volume 952 of *LNCS*, pages 253–282, Aarhus, Denmark, August 1995. Springer-Verlag. doi:10.1007/3-540-49538-X_13.

[48] Stéphane Ducasse. Evaluating message passing control techniques in Smalltalk. *Journal of Object-Oriented Programming (JOOP)*, 12(6):39–44, June 1999. Available from: http://scg.unibe.ch/archive/papers/Duca99aMsgPassingControl.pdf.

[49] Stéphane Ducasse, Oscar Nierstrasz, Nathanael Schärli, Roel Wuyts, and Andrew P. Black. Traits: A mechanism for fine-grained reuse. *ACM Transactions on Programming Languages and Systems (TOPLAS)*, 28(2):331–388, March 2006. Available from: http://scg.unibe.ch/archive/papers/Duca06bTOPLASTraits.pdf, doi:10.1145/1119479.1119483.

[50] Dwarf debugging standard. Available from: http://dwarfstd.org/.

[51] Peter Ebraert, Jorge Vallejos, Pascal Costanza, Ellen Van Paesschen, and Theo D'Hondt. Change-oriented software engineering. In *Proceedings of the 2007 international conference on Dynamic languages: in conjunction with the 15th International Smalltalk Joint Conference 2007*, ICDL '07, pages 3–24, New York, NY, USA, 2007. ACM.

[52] Sebastian Erdweg, Lennart C.L. Kats, Tillmann Rendel, Christian Kästner, Klaus Ostermann, and Eelco Visser. Library-based model-driven software development with sugarj. In *Proceedings of the ACM international conference companion on Object oriented programming systems languages and applications companion*, SPLASH '11, pages 17–18, New York, NY, USA, 2011. ACM. doi:10.1145/2048147.2048156.

[53] M. Anton Ertl and David Gregg. The behavior of efficient virtual machine interpreters on modern architectures. In *Proceedings of the 7th International Euro-Par Conference Manchester on Parallel Processing*, Euro-Par '01, pages 403–412, London, UK, 2001. Springer-Verlag. Available from: http://dl.acm.org/citation.cfm?id=646666.699857.

[54] M. Anton Ertl and David Gregg. Optimizing indirect branch prediction accuracy in virtual machine interpreters. *SIGPLAN Not.*, 38:278–288, May 2003. doi:10.1145/780822.781162.

[55] M. Anton Ertl and David Gregg. The structure and performance of efficient interpreters. *Journal of Instruction-Level Parallelism*, 5, 2003. Available from: http://www.jilp.org/vol5/v5paper12.pdf.

[56] M. Anton Ertl, David Gregg, Andreas Krall, and Bernd Paysan. vmgen — a generator of efficient virtual machine interpreters. *Software — Practice and Experience*, 2002.

[57] Glauber Ferreira, Emerson Loureiro, and Elthon Oliveira. A Java code annotation approach for model checking software systems. In *Proceedings of the 2007 ACM symposium on Applied computing*, SAC '07, pages 1536–1537, New York, NY, USA, 2007. ACM. doi:10.1145/1244002.1244330.

[58] Jeffrey Fischer, Daniel Marino, Rupak Majumdar, and Todd Millstein. Fine-grained access control with object-sensitive roles. In *Proceedings of the 23rd European Conference on ECOOP 2009 — Object-Oriented Programming*, Genoa, pages 173–194, Berlin, Heidelberg, 2009. Springer-Verlag. doi:10.1007/978-3-642-03013-0_9.

[59] David Flanagan. *JavaScript: The Definitive Guide*. O'Reilly & Associates, second edition, January 1997. Available from: http://www.ora.com/catalog/jscript2/noframes.html.

[60] Brian Foote and Ralph E. Johnson. Reflective facilities in Smalltalk-80. In *Proceedings OOPSLA '89, ACM SIGPLAN Notices*, volume 24, pages 327–336, October 1989.

[61] Bryan Ford. Parsing expression grammars: a recognition-based syntactic foundation. In *POPL '04: Proceedings of the 31st ACM SIGPLAN-SIGACT symposium on Principles of programming languages*, pages 111–122, New York, NY, USA, 2004. ACM. Available from: http://pdos.csail.mit.edu/~baford/packrat/popl04/peg-popl04.pdf, doi:10.1145/964001.964011.

[62] Martin Fowler. Inversion of control containers and the dependency injection pattern. http://martinfowler.com/articles/injection.html archived at http://www.webcitation.org/5wLOsI8ov, January 2004. Available from: http://www.webcitation.org/5wLOsI8ov.

[63] Martin Fowler. Language workbenches: The killer-app for domain-specific languages, June 2005. Available from: http://www.martinfowler.com/articles/languageWorkbench.html.

[64] Michael Franz and Thomas Kistler. Slim binaries. *Commun. ACM*, 40(12):87–94, 1997. doi:10.1145/265563.265576.

[65] Adele Goldberg and David Robson. *Smalltalk 80: the Language and its Implementation*. Addison Wesley, Reading, Mass., May 1983. Available from: http://stephane.ducasse.free.fr/FreeBooks/BlueBook/Bluebook.pdf.

[66] Groovy. http://groovy.codehaus.org/.

[67] David Grove, Jeffrey Dean, Charles Garrett, and Craig Chambers. Profile-guided receiver class prediction. In *Proceedings of the tenth annual conference on Object-oriented programming systems, languages, and*

applications, OOPSLA '95, pages 108–123, New York, NY, USA, 1995. ACM. doi:10.1145/217838.217848.

[68] Kris Gybels, Roel Wuyts, Stéphane Ducasse, and Maja D'Hondt. Inter-language reflection — a conceptual model and its implementation. *Journal of Computer Languages, Systems and Structures*, 32(2-3):109–124, July 2006. Available from: http://scg.unibe.ch/archive/papers/Gybe06aSymbioticReflectionESUGJournal.pdf, doi:10.1016/j.cl.2005.10.003.

[69] Tim Harris and Keir Fraser. Language support for lightweight transactions. In *Object-Oriented Programming, Systems, Languages, and Applications*, pages 388–402. ACM Press, New York, NY, USA, October 2003. doi:10.1145/949305.949340.

[70] Michael Haupt, Bram Adams, Stijn Timbermont, Celina Gibbs, Yvonne Coady, and Robert Hirschfeld. Disentangling virtual machine architecture. *IET Software*, 3(3):201–218, 2009. doi:10.1049/iet-sen.2007.0121.

[71] Christopher T. Haynes, Daniel P. Friedman, and Mitchell Wand. Continuations and coroutines. In *LFP '84: Proceedings of the 1984 ACM Symposium on LISP and functional programming*, pages 293–298, New York, NY, USA, 1984. ACM. doi:10.1145/800055.802046.

[72] Rich Hickey. The Clojure programming language. In *DLS '08: Proceedings of the 2008 symposium on Dynamic languages*, pages 1–1, New York, NY, USA, 2008. ACM. Available from: http://doi.acm.org/10.1145/1408681.1408682, doi:10.1145/1408681.1408682.

[73] Michael Hicks and Scott Nettles. Dynamic software updating. *ACM Transactions on Programming Languages and Systems*, 27(6):1049–1096, nov 2005. doi:10.1145/1108970.1108971.

[74] Urs Hölzle, Craig Chambers, and David Ungar. Optimizing dynamically-typed object-oriented languages with polymorphic inline caches. In P. America, editor, *Proceedings ECOOP '91*, volume 512 of *LNCS*, pages 21–38, Geneva, Switzerland, July 1991. Springer-Verlag. doi:10.1007/BFb0057013.

[75] Urs Hölzle and David Ungar. Optimizing dynamically-dispatched calls with run-time type feedback. In *Proceedings of the ACM SIGPLAN 1994 conference on Programming language design and implementation*, PLDI '94, pages 326–336, New York, NY, USA, 1994. ACM. doi:10.1145/178243.178478.

[76] Paul Hudak. Modular domain specific languages and tools. In P. Devanbu and J. Poulin, editors, *Proceedings: Fifth International Conference on Software Reuse*, pages 134–142. IEEE Computer Society Press, 1998.

[77] Mamdouh H. Ibrahim. Reflection and metalevel architectures in object-oriented programming (workshop session). In *OOPSLA/ECOOP '90: Proceedings of the European conference on Object-oriented programming addendum: systems, languages, and applications*, pages 73–80, New York, NY, USA, 1991. ACM Press. doi:10.1145/319016.319050.

[78] Dan Ingalls, Ted Kaehler, John Maloney, Scott Wallace, and Alan Kay. Back to the future: The story of Squeak, a practical Smalltalk written in itself. In *OOPSLA'97: Proceedings of the 12th International Conference on Object-Oriented Programming, Systems, Languages, and Applications*, pages 318–326. ACM Press, November 1997. Available from: http://www.cosc.canterbury.ac.nz/~wolfgang/cosc205/squeak.html, doi:10.1145/263700.263754.

[79] Tor E. Jeremiassen and Susan J. Eggers. Reducing false sharing on shared memory multiprocessors through compile time data transformations. In *Proceedings of the fifth ACM SIGPLAN symposium on Principles and practice of parallel programming*, PPOPP '95, pages 179–188, New York, NY, USA, 1995. ACM. doi:10.1145/209936.209955.

[80] The Jikes research virtual machine. Available from: http://jikesrvm.sourceforge.net/.

[81] Joel Jones. Abstract syntax tree implementation idioms. In *Pattern Languages of Programs*, September 2003. Available from: http://hillside.net/plop/plop2003/Papers/Jones-ImplementingASTs.pdf.

[82] JRuby. Available from: http://www.jruby.org/.

[83] Stephen Kell and Conrad Irwin. Virtual machines should be invisible. In *VMIL '11: Proceedings of the 5th workshop on Virtual machines and intermediate languages for emerging modularization mechanisms*, page 6. ACM, 2011. Available from: http://www.cs.iastate.edu/~design/vmil/2011/papers/p02-kell.pdf.

[84] Gregor Kiczales. Beyond the black box: Open implementation. *IEEE Software*, January 1996.

[85] Gregor Kiczales, Jim des Rivières, and Daniel G. Bobrow. *The Art of the Metaobject Protocol*. MIT Press, 1991.

[86] Gregor Kiczales, Erik Hilsdale, Jim Hugunin, Mik Kersten, Jeffrey Palm, and William G. Griswold. An overview of AspectJ. In *Proceedings ECOOP 2001*, number 2072 in LNCS, pages 327–353. Springer Verlag, 2001.

[87] Gregor Kiczales, John Lamping, Anurag Mendhekar, Chris Maeda, Cristina Lopes, Jean-Marc Loingtier, and John Irwin. Aspect-oriented programming. In Mehmet Aksit and Satoshi Matsuoka,

editors, *ECOOP'97: Proceedings of the 11th European Conference on Object-Oriented Programming*, volume 1241 of *LNCS*, pages 220–242, Jyvaskyla, Finland, June 1997. Springer-Verlag. doi:10.1007/BFb0053381.

[88] Thomas Kotzmann and Hanspeter Mössenböck. Escape analysis in the context of dynamic compilation and deoptimization. In *Proceedings of the 1st ACM/USENIX international conference on Virtual execution environments*, VEE '05, pages 111–120, New York, NY, USA, 2005. ACM. doi:10.1145/1064979.1064996.

[89] Glenn Krasner. *Smalltalk-80: Bits of History, Words of Advice*. Addison Wesley, Reading, Mass., 1983. Available from: http://stephane.ducasse.free.fr/FreeBooks/BitsOfHistory/BitsOfHistory.pdf.

[90] Wilf R. LaLonde and Mark Van Gulik. Building a backtracking facility in Smalltalk without kernel support. In *Proceedings OOPSLA '88, ACM SIGPLAN Notices*, volume 23, pages 105–122, November 1988. doi:10.1145/62083.62094.

[91] Xavier Leroy. Java bytecode verification: An overview. In Gérard Berry, Hubert Comon, and Alain Finkel, editors, *Computer Aided Verification*, volume 2102 of *Lecture Notes in Computer Science*, pages 265–285. Springer Berlin / Heidelberg, 2001. doi:10.1007/3-540-44585-4_26.

[92] Adrian Lienhard. *Dynamic Object Flow Analysis*. Phd thesis, University of Bern, December 2008. Available from: http://scg.unibe.ch/archive/phd/lienhard-phd.pdf.

[93] Adrian Lienhard, Stéphane Ducasse, Tudor Gîrba, and Oscar Nierstrasz. Capturing how objects flow at runtime. In *Proceedings International Workshop on Program Comprehension through Dynamic Analysis (PCODA'06)*, pages 39–43, 2006. Available from: http://scg.unibe.ch/archive/papers/Lien06aCapturingHowObjectsFlowPCODA06.pdf.

[94] Adrian Lienhard, Tudor Gîrba, and Oscar Nierstrasz. Practical object-oriented back-in-time debugging. In *Proceedings of the 22nd European Conference on Object-Oriented Programming (ECOOP'08)*, volume 5142 of *LNCS*, pages 592–615. Springer, 2008. ECOOP distinguished paper award. Available from: http://scg.unibe.ch/archive/papers/Lien08bBackInTimeDebugging.pdf, doi:10.1007/978-3-540-70592-5_25.

[95] Pattie Maes. Concepts and experiments in computational reflection. In *Proceedings OOPSLA '87, ACM SIGPLAN Notices*, volume 22, pages 147–155, December 1987. doi:10.1145/38765.38821.

[96] Scott Malabarba, Raju Pandey, Jeff Gragg, Earl Barr, and J. Fritz Barnes. Runtime support for type-safe dynamic Java classes. In *Proceedings of the 14th European Conference on Object-Oriented Programming*, pages 337–361. Springer-Verlag, 2000. doi:10.1007/3-540-45102-1_17.

[97] Jacques Malenfant, Christophe Dony, and Pierre Cointe. Behavioral Reflection in a prototype-based language. In A. Yonezawa and B. Smith, editors, *Proceedings of Int'l Workshop on Reflection and Meta-Level Architectures*, pages 143–153, Tokyo, November 1992. RISE and IPA(Japan) + ACM SIGPLAN.

[98] Jacques Malenfant, M. Jacques, and François-Nicolas Demers. A tutorial on behavioral reflection and its implementation. In *Proceedings of Reflection*, pages 1–20, 1996. Available from: http://www2.parc.com/csl/groups/sda/projects/reflection96/docs/malenfant/malenfant.pdf.

[99] Jeff McAffer. *A Meta-level Architecture for Prototyping Object Systems*. Ph.D. thesis, University of Tokyo, September 1995. Available from: http://www.laputan.org/pub/mcaffer/mcaffer-phd.pdf.

[100] Jeff McAffer. Engineering the meta level. In Gregor Kiczales, editor, *Proceedings of the 1st International Conference on Metalevel Architectures and Reflection (Reflection 96)*, San Francisco, USA, April 1996.

[101] Erik Meijer, Brian Beckman, and Gavin Bierman. LINQ: reconciling object, relations and XML in the .NET framework. In *SIGMOD '06: Proceedings of the 2006 ACM SIGMOD international conference on Management of data*, pages 706–706, New York, NY, USA, 2006. ACM. doi:10.1145/1142473.1142552.

[102] Erik Meijer and John Gough. Technical overview of the common language runtime, 2001. Available from: http://dforeman.cs.binghamton.edu/~foreman/552pages/Readings/meijer.pdf.

[103] Mark Samuel Miller. *Robust Composition: Towards a Unified Approach to Access Control and Concurrency Control*. PhD thesis, Johns Hopkins University, Baltimore, Maryland, USA, May 2006. Available from: http://e-drexler.com/d/06/00/robust_composition.pdf.

[104] Eliot Miranda. Brouhaha — A portable Smalltalk interpreter. In *Proceedings OOPSLA '87, ACM SIGPLAN Notices*, volume 22, pages 354–365, December 1987.

[105] Eliot Miranda. Portable fast direct threaded code, 1991. Available from: http://compilers.iecc.com/comparch/article/91-03-121.

[106] Eliot Miranda. Context management in VisualWorks 5i. Technical report, ParcPlace Division, CINCOM, Inc., 1999.

[107] Iulian Neamtiu, Michael Hicks, Gareth Stoyle, and Manuel Oriol. Practical dynamic software updating for C. In *Proceedings of the 2006 ACM SIGPLAN conference on Programming language design and implementation*, PLDI '06, pages 72–83, New York, NY, USA, 2006. ACM. Available from: http://doi.acm.org/10.1145/1133981.1133991, doi:10.1145/1133981.1133991.

[108] Oscar Nierstrasz. Putting change at the center of the software process. In I. Crnkovic, J.A. Stafford, H.W. Schmidt, and K. Wallnau, editors, *International Symposium on Component-Based Software Engineering (CBSE) 2004*, volume 3054 of *LNCS*, pages 1–4. Springer-Verlag, 2004. Extended abstract of an invited talk. Available from: http://scg.unibe.ch/archive/papers/Nier04bChange.pdf, doi:10.1007/b97813.

[109] Oscar Nierstrasz, Alexandre Bergel, Marcus Denker, Stéphane Ducasse, Markus Gaelli, and Roel Wuyts. On the revival of dynamic languages. In Thomas Gschwind and Uwe Aßmann, editors, *Proceedings of Software Composition 2005*, volume 3628, pages 1–13. LNCS 3628, 2005. Invited paper. Available from: http://scg.unibe.ch/archive/papers/Nier05bRevival.pdf, doi:10.1007/11550679_1.

[110] Alessandro Orso, Anup Rao, and Mary Jean Harrold. A Technique for Dynamic Updating of Java Software. *Software Maintenance, IEEE International Conference on*, 0:0649+, 2002. Available from: http://dx.doi.org/10.1109/ICSM.2002.1167829, doi:10.1109/ICSM.2002.1167829.

[111] Andreas Paepcke. PCLOS: Stress testing CLOS experiencing the metaobject protocol. In *Proceedings OOPSLA/ECOOP '90, ACM SIGPLAN Notices*, volume 25, pages 194–211, October 1990.

[112] Andreas Paepcke. User-level language crafting. In *Object-Oriented Programming: the CLOS perspective*, pages 66–99. MIT Press, 1993.

[113] Mike Pall. Why the LuaJIT interpreter is written in assembler, 2011. Available from: http://article.gmane.org/gmane.comp.lang.lua.general/75426.

[114] D. Jason Penney and Jacob Stein. Class modification in the gemstone object-oriented DBMS. In *Proceedings OOPSLA '87, ACM SIGPLAN Notices*, volume 22, pages 111–117, December 1987.

[115] Ian Piumarta. Accessible language-based environments of recursive theories (a white paper advocating widespread unreasonable behavior). Technical report, Viewpoints Research Institute, 2006. VPRI Research Note RN-2006-001-a. Available from: http://vpri.org/pdf/rn2006001a_colaswp.pdf.

[116] Ian Piumarta and Fabio Riccardi. Optimizing direct threaded code by selective inlining. In *Proceedings of the ACM SIGPLAN 1998 conference on Programming language design and implementation*, PLDI '98, pages 291–300, New York, NY, USA, 1998. ACM. doi:10.1145/277650.277743.

[117] Ian Piumarta and Alessandro Warth. Open reusable object models. Technical report, Viewpoints Research Institute, 2006. VPRI Research Note RN-2006-003-a. Available from: http://vpri.org/pdf/tr2006003a_objmod.pdf.

[118] Massimiliano Poletto and Vivek Sarkar. Linear scan register allocation. *ACM Trans. Program. Lang. Syst.*, 21:895–913, sep 1999. doi:10.1145/330249.330250.

[119] Python. http://www.python.org.

[120] Barry Redmond and Vinny Cahill. Iguana/J: Towards a dynamic and efficient reflective architecture for Java. In *Proceedings of European Conference on Object-Oriented Programming, workshop on Reflection and Meta-Level Architectures*, 2000.

[121] Lukas Renggli, Stéphane Ducasse, and Adrian Kuhn. Magritte — a meta-driven approach to empower developers and end users. In Gregor Engels, Bill Opdyke, Douglas C. Schmidt, and Frank Weil, editors, *Model Driven Engineering Languages and Systems*, volume 4735 of *LNCS*, pages 106–120. Springer, September 2007. Available from: http://scg.unibe.ch/archive/papers/Reng07aMagritte.pdf, doi:10.1007/978-3-540-75209-7_8.

[122] Lukas Renggli, Tudor Gîrba, and Oscar Nierstrasz. Embedding languages without breaking tools. In Theo D'Hondt, editor, *ECOOP'10: Proceedings of the 24th European Conference on Object-Oriented Programming*, volume 6183 of *LNCS*, pages 380–404, Maribor, Slovenia, 2010. Springer-Verlag. Available from: http://scg.unibe.ch/archive/papers/Reng10aEmbeddingLanguages.pdf, doi:10.1007/978-3-642-14107-2_19.

[123] Armin Rigo and Samuele Pedroni. PyPy's approach to virtual machine construction. In *Proceedings of the 2006 conference on Dynamic languages symposium, OOPSLA '06: Companion to the 21st ACM SIGPLAN conference on Object-oriented programming systems, languages, and applications*, pages 944–953, New York, NY, USA, 2006. ACM. doi:10.1145/1176617.1176753.

[124] Fred Rivard. Smalltalk: a reflective language. In *Proceedings of REFLECTION '96*, pages 21–38, April 1996.

[125] Romain Robbes. *Of Change and Software*. PhD thesis, University of Lugano, December 2008. Available from: http://www.inf.unisi.ch/phd/robbes/OfChangeAndSoftware.pdf.

[126] Leonardo Rodríguez, Éric Tanter, and Jacques Noyé. Supporting dynamic crosscutting with partial behavioral reflection: a case study. In *Proceedings of the XXIV International Conference of the Chilean Computer Science Society (SCCC 2004)*, Arica, Chile, November 2004. IEEE.

[127] David Röthlisberger, Marcus Denker, and Éric Tanter. Unanticipated partial behavioral reflection. In *Advances in Smalltalk — Proceedings of 14th International Smalltalk Conference (ISC 2006)*, volume 4406 of *LNCS*, pages 47–65. Springer, 2007. Available from: http://scg.unibe.ch/archive/papers/Roet07bUPBReflection.pdf, doi:10.1007/978-3-540-71836-9_3.

[128] The Scala programming language. http://lamp.epfl.ch/scala/. Available from: http://lamp.epfl.ch/scala/.

[129] Niko Schwarz, Mircea Lungu, and Oscar Nierstrasz. Seuss: Cleaning up class responsibilities with language-based dependency injection. In *Objects, Components, Models and Patterns, Proceedings of TOOLS Europe 2011*, volume 33 of *LNCS*, pages 276–289. Springer-Verlag, 2011. Available from: http://scg.unibe.ch/archive/papers/Schw11aSeuss.pdf, doi:10.1007/978-3-642-21952-8_20.

[130] Mark E. Segal and Ophir Frieder. On-the-fly program modification: Systems for dynamic updating. *IEEE Softw.*, 10(2):53–65, 1993. Available from: http://dx.doi.org/10.1109/52.199735, doi:10.1109/52.199735.

[131] Julian Seward and Nicholas Nethercote. Using Valgrind to detect undefined value errors with bit-precision. In *Proceedings of the annual conference on USENIX Annual Technical Conference*, ATEC '05, pages 2–2, Berkeley, CA, USA, 2005. USENIX Association.

[132] Yunhe Shi, Kevin Casey, M. Anton Ertl, and David Gregg. Virtual machine showdown: Stack versus registers. *ACM Trans. Archit. Code Optim.*, 4:2:1–2:36, January 2008. doi:10.1145/1328195.1328197.

[133] John W. Simmons, Stanley Jefferson, and Daniel P. Friedman. Language extension via first-class interpreters. Technical Report 362, Indiana University Computer Science Department, September 1992. Available from: http://www.cs.indiana.edu/pub/techreports/TR362.pdf.

[134] Brian Cantwell Smith. *Reflection and Semantics in a Procedural Language*. Ph.D. thesis, MIT, Cambridge, MA, 1982. Available from: http://repository.readscheme.org/ftp/papers/bcsmith-thesis.pdf.

[135] Marc Stiegler. The E language in a walnut, 2004. Available from: www.skyhunter.com/marcs/ewalnut.html.

[136] Anselm Strauss. Dynamic aspects — an AOP implementation for Squeak. Master's thesis, University of Bern, November 2008. Available from: http://scg.unibe.ch/archive/masters/Strau08a.pdf.

[137] Suriya Subramanian, Michael Hicks, and Kathryn S. McKinley. Dynamic software updates: a VM-centric approach. In *Proceedings of the 2009 ACM SIGPLAN conference on Programming language design and implementation*, PLDI '09, pages 1–12, New York, NY, USA, 2009. ACM. Available from: http://doi.acm.org/10.1145/1542476.1542478, doi:10.1145/1542476.1542478.

[138] Sun microsystems. Java annotations, 2004. Available from: http://java.sun.com/j2se/1.5.0/docs/guide/language/annotations.html.

[139] Éric Tanter. Contextual values. In *Proceedings of the 2008 symposium on Dynamic languages*, DLS '08, pages 3:1–3:10, New York, NY, USA, 2008. ACM. doi:10.1145/1408681.1408684.

[140] Éric Tanter. Reflection and open implementations. Technical Report TR/DCC-2009-13, University of Chile, November 2009. Available from: http://www.dcc.uchile.cl/TR/2009/TR_DCC-20091123-013.pdf.

[141] Éric Tanter, Jacques Noyé, Denis Caromel, and Pierre Cointe. Partial behavioral reflection: Spatial and temporal selection of reification. In *Proceedings of OOPSLA '03, ACM SIGPLAN Notices*, pages 27–46, nov 2003. Available from: http://www.dcc.uchile.cl/~etanter/research/publi/2003/tanter-oopsla03.pdf, doi:10.1145/949305.949309.

[142] David Ungar and Randall B. Smith. Self: The power of simplicity. In *Proceedings OOPSLA '87, ACM SIGPLAN Notices*, volume 22, pages 227–242, December 1987. doi:10.1145/38765.38828.

[143] David Ungar, Adam Spitz, and Alex Ausch. Constructing a metacircular virtual machine in an exploratory programming environment. In *OOPSLA '05: Companion to the 20th annual ACM SIGPLAN conference on Object-oriented programming, systems, languages, and applications*, pages 11–20, New York, NY, USA, 2005. ACM. doi:10.1145/1094855.1094865.

[144] David M Ungar. *The Design and Evaluation of A High Performance Smalltalk System*. PhD thesis, University of California at Berkeley, Berkeley, CA, USA, 1986.

[145] Toon Verwaest, Camillo Bruni, David Gurtner, Adrian Lienhard, and Oscar Nierstrasz. Pinocchio: Bringing reflection to life with first-class interpreters. In *OOPSLA Onward!* '10, volume 45, pages 774–789, New York, NY, USA, 2010. ACM. Available from: http://scg.unibe.ch/archive/papers/Verw10aPinocchio.pdf, doi:10.1145/1869459.1869522.

[146] Toon Verwaest, Camillo Bruni, Mircea Lungu, and Oscar Nierstrasz. Flexible object layouts: enabling lightweight language extensions by intercepting slot access. In *Proceedings of the 2011 ACM international conference on Object oriented programming systems languages and applications*, OOPSLA '11, pages 959–972, New York, NY, USA, 2011. ACM. Available from: http://scg.unibe.ch/archive/papers/Verw11bFlexibleObjectLayouts.pdf, doi:10.1145/2048066.2048138.

[147] Toon Verwaest, Niko Schwarz, and Erwann Wernli. Runtime class updates using modification models. In *Proceedings of the TOOLS 2011 8th Workshop on Reflection, AOP and Meta-Data for Software Evolution (RAM-SE'11)*, 2011. Available from: http://scg.unibe.ch/archive/papers/Verw11aRuntimeUpdates.pdf.

[148] Mitchell Wand and Daniel Friedman. The Mystery of the Tower Revealed: A Non-Reflective Description of the Reflective Tower. In P. Maes North-Holland and D. Nardi, editors, *Meta-level Architectures and Reflection*, pages 111–134, 1988.

[149] Tobias Wrigstad, Patrick Eugster, John Field, Nate Nystrom, and Jan Vitek. Software hardening: a research agenda. In *Proceedings for the 1st workshop on Script to Program Evolution*, STOP '09, pages 58–70, New York, NY, USA, 2009. ACM. doi:10.1145/1570506.1570513.

[150] Roel Wuyts and Stéphane Ducasse. Symbiotic reflection between an object-oriented and a logic programming language. In *ECOOP 2001 International Workshop on MultiParadigm Programming with Object-Oriented Languages*, 2001. Available from: http://scg.unibe.ch/archive/papers/Wuyt01a.pdf.

[151] Alexander Yermolovich, Christian Wimmer, and Michael Franz. Optimization of dynamic languages using hierarchical layering of virtual machines. In *Proceedings of the 5th symposium on Dynamic languages*, DLS '09, pages 79–88, New York, NY, USA, 2009. ACM. doi:10.1145/1640134.1640147.

Curriculum Vitae

Personal Information

Name: Toon Verwaest
Date of Birth: February 07, 1984
Place of Birth: Turnhout, Belgium
Nationality: Belgian

Education

2007–2012 **PhD in Computer Science**
Software Composition Group,
University of Bern, Switzerland
http://scg.unibe.ch

2006–2007 **EMOOSE**
European Master in Object-, Component-, and
Aspect-Oriented Software Engineering Technologies,
5 months at École de Mines de Nantes, France,
6 months at Universidad Nacional de La Plata, Argentina.
http://www.emn.fr/emoose

2004–2006 **Master of Science in Theoretical Computer Science**,
University, Vrije Universiteit Brussel, Belgium,
Graduated with Distinction in July of 2006.
http://www.vub.ac.be

www.ingramcontent.com/pod-product-compliance
Lightning Source LLC
Chambersburg PA
CBHW021959170526
45157CB00003B/1058